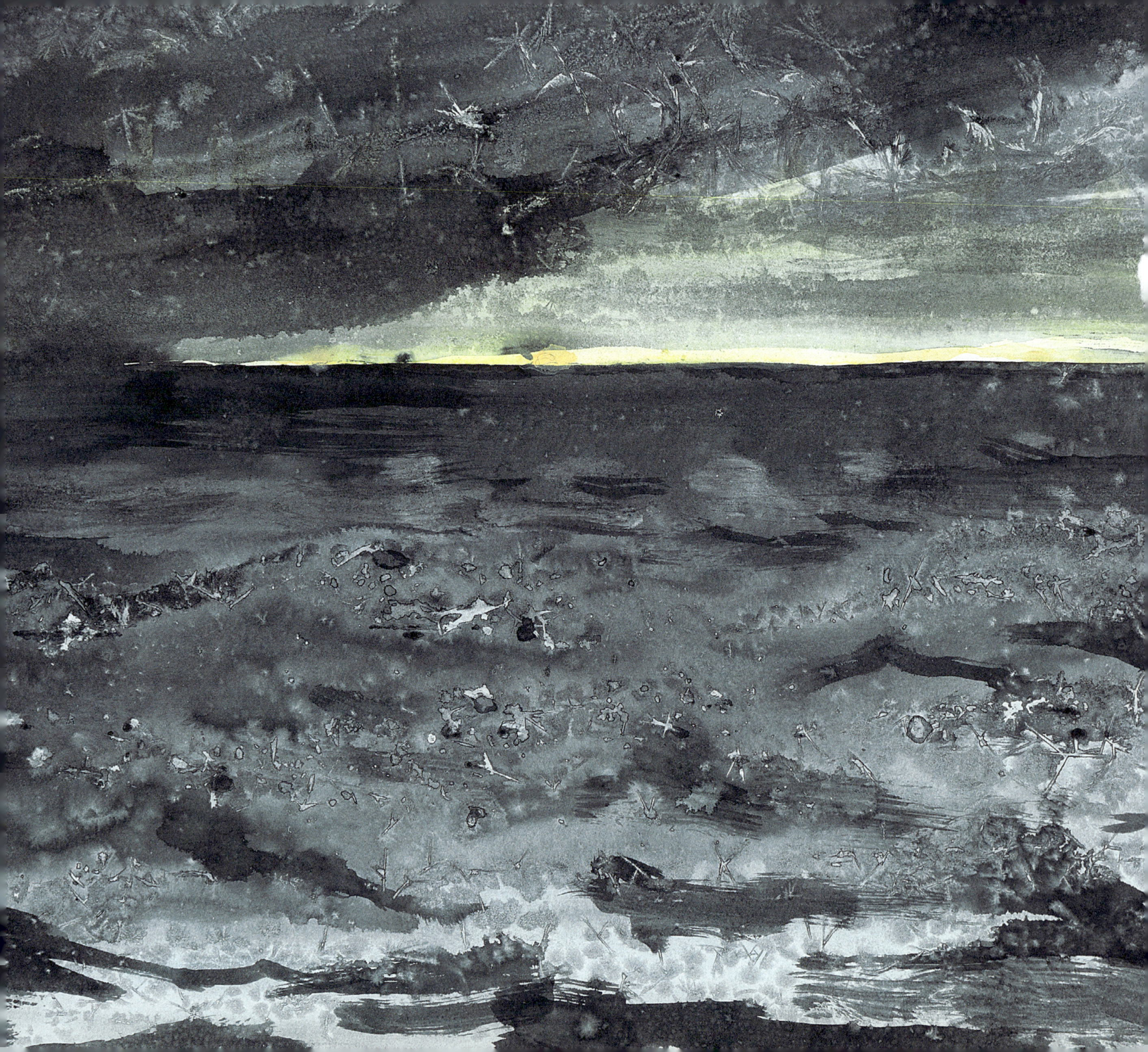

Emma Stibbon

MELTING ICE RISING TIDES

TOWNER Eastbourne | Royal Academy of Arts

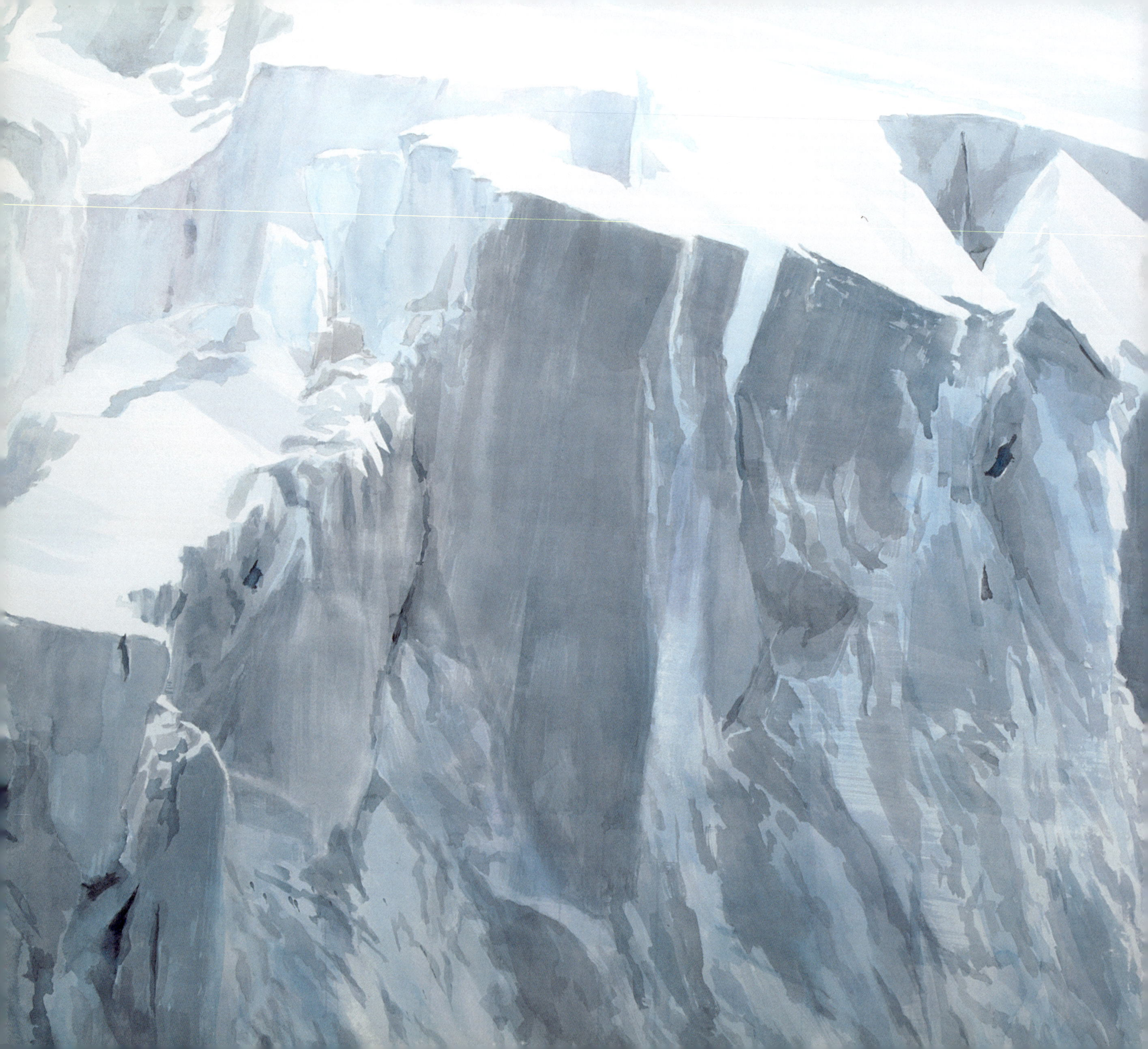

CONTENTS

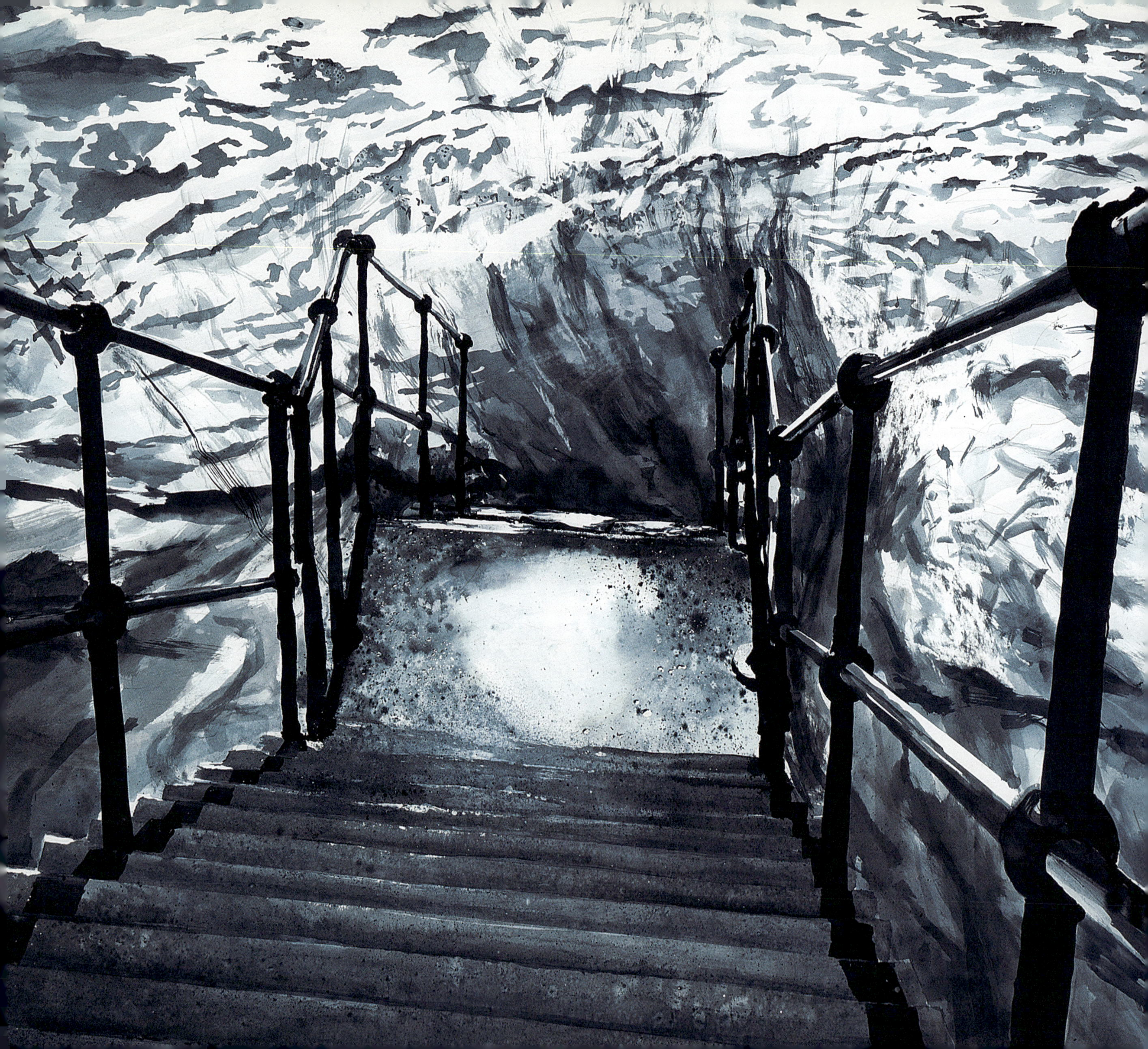

FOREWORD

Caroline Lucas MP

There is a raw, savage beauty in Emma Stibbon's work that simultaneously captures both the permanence and the fragility of the natural world. The stark rock faces and the roiling seas seem like they have been, and will be, there forever. Yet we know that the landscapes we see today are changing in our lifetimes as a direct result of human activity, whether it's melting ice at the polar regions or the accelerating erosion of our own stunning Sussex coastline. So when I look at Emma's work, I find myself asking what those landscapes will look like in 50 years' time? Will that glacier still be there? Or that cliff face? Will families still be playing on that beach, or walking along that clifftop? What will future generations see when they stand on the same spot – if indeed that same spot even still exists?

This sense of the familiar becoming unfamiliar was also the inspiration behind an exhibition I had the privilege of curating at Towner Eastbourne four years ago, which drew on the wonderful collection of landscapes at the gallery. The exhibition was called 'Brink', to reflect the sense of being on the edge of massive, irreversible change, because while we've been warned about the accelerating climate emergency for decades and have reams of scientific data setting out the deadly impact of our actions, it has failed to lead to the political and economic changes we so urgently need. We don't lack facts or evidence about the climate crisis. What's lacking is the political will to act, and this is at least partly because of a devastating failure of imagination: it seems that we simply don't grasp what we're doing to our collective home – or if we do, we don't believe there's anything we as individuals can do to change it.

This is what makes the work of artists like Emma Stibbon, and her exhibition 'Melting Ice | Rising Tides', so important. They help us to connect with the world around us and *feel* – emotionally and viscerally – the reality of what we're doing in ways that can be far more effective than a political speech or a campaign leaflet. Emma's work feeds our imagination, inspires us to act, and shows us that each and every one of us can make a difference.

MELTING
ICE
RISING
TIDES

**Emma Stibbon in conversation
with Sara Cooper**

The new work you have produced for 'Melting Ice / Rising Tides' is expansive in its scope, looking at both local and global landscapes. Could you explain what led you to make it?
I've recently been thinking about how I can make work that is geographically and materially related. My ideas came together when I was given the opportunity to show my work in this solo exhibition at Towner Eastbourne, a venue situated close to the chalk downlands of East Sussex. This coastline is prone to cliff failure and losses that are increasing each year due to wave erosion and extreme weather.[1] I want viewers to experience a strong sense of place recognition through locations that are familiar, displayed alongside the icy terrains of the polar regions, where ice melt is contributing to a global rise in sea levels.[2] We can see very clearly along the UK's shores the effects of coastal erosion caused by extreme weather, but it's hard to envisage that these local events are connected to seemingly remote melting ice sheets and glaciers at the extremities of our planet.

You've worked in some remote landscapes, among them volcanic regions, and you frequently work in frozen or glaciated landscapes. What attracts you to these places?
I have an enduring fascination with extreme, particularly cold places, and I want to record their incredible wonder and beauty. But this of course is now underscored by an awareness of their instability due to a rapidly warming environment. Scientific data shows how the increasing melt of glaciers and ice sheets is having a profound effect on our global environment through rising sea levels. As an artist who works from the landscape, I'm increasingly committed to documenting these events in my work.

For this body of work you're focusing on the sea. What drew you to this subject matter now?
I wanted to suggest how fundamental the sea is to our global interconnectedness. Now that ocean currents are changing due to warming seas it seems almost counterintuitive that ice losses from the Arctic are having the greatest impact on lower latitudes such as South America. It's difficult to hold this immense image in our minds. By bringing together these geographical expanses visually I want to suggest our co-dependence; that we are joined together by the oceans.

You've recently visited the polar regions. What does this field experience bring to the project?
I feel an imperative to draw in the landscape, to root my work in that physical, visceral experience of being in a place. As part of my research, I visited Antarctica in early 2023. Witnessing the vast icy expanses of the Weddell Sea I was awed by the massive tabular bergs. It's disorientating to see these majestic continents of ice, and impossible to estimate their size. As I was drawing in my sketchbook, I was trying to record the character of each berg as it passed our ship. Often it would change before my eyes, breaking up or rotating due to its instability. I wanted to record the particularities of each berg, to pay homage to something ephemeral and fleeting.

We've included some of your sketchbook drawings in the exhibition, shifting them from what might be considered your personal workings into something public. How do you use your sketchbooks? What is their function in your process?
I don't usually show my sketchbook drawings. They are a more personal space that I refer to in the studio when I'm making my larger works. They hold a sense of being in a place that reminds me of the experience. Drawing from observation has a very immediate dynamic, unlike drawing in the studio. There's the urgency of the changing weather and there are the challenges of working in the cold – often my watercolours and inks freeze on the page. That physical experience of battling in the elements becomes part of the drawing and is often apparent when snow or rain spot the media on the page. It's surprising to me that when I review my on-site sketches I have such vivid recall of a place, the weather and time of day – even how I was feeling.

This is evident in your series of drawings of the Barents Sea, where the weather actually found its way into the drawings. Can you talk about how they were made?
In April 2022 I travelled with a group of artists on a wooden barquentine sailing vessel from northern Norway to Svalbard in the High Arctic.[3] Despite the bad weather the captain eventually decided that we could make the three-day voyage north across the Barents Sea. I sat out on deck making a series of A4-sized ink drawings (pp. 52–53) of the different weather conditions and atmospherics of the rough sea – mostly to distract myself from being seasick. As we sailed north, the air temperatures dropped and my watery drawing ink started to freeze, causing ice-crystal patterns to form on the paper. I was also helping the crew by recording the sea temperature and latitudes in the ship's log. Later, back in the studio, I compared the log information to my dated drawings and realised that the weather was literally physically recorded in my drawing media by latitude as we tracked our northerly course.

You often incorporate materials gathered from your working locations into your drawing media. Why is this?
I love the directness and simplicity of drawing, and the thought that I can pick up something from the ground or extract material elements from my surroundings and make marks with them. When drawing the chalk cliffs of East Sussex, for example, it was obvious to work with the chalk that was so abundant on the beach. Some of my drawing locations are literally perched on the edge of a chalk cliff, like the coastguard cottages at Birling Gap (2023; pp. 63 and 65). It seemed appropriate to introduce ground chalk from the cliff into the drawings, in this case works in fragile chalk on black prepared paper. I'm interested in the way the chalk represents the elusiveness of the subject; it could literally be wiped away with your hand. For my large drawing of the sea, *Breaker* (2023; pp. 54–55), I used Sussex sea water to dilute my ink and added sea salt to the darker washes. Surprisingly, this dispersed the ink in a peculiar way that can

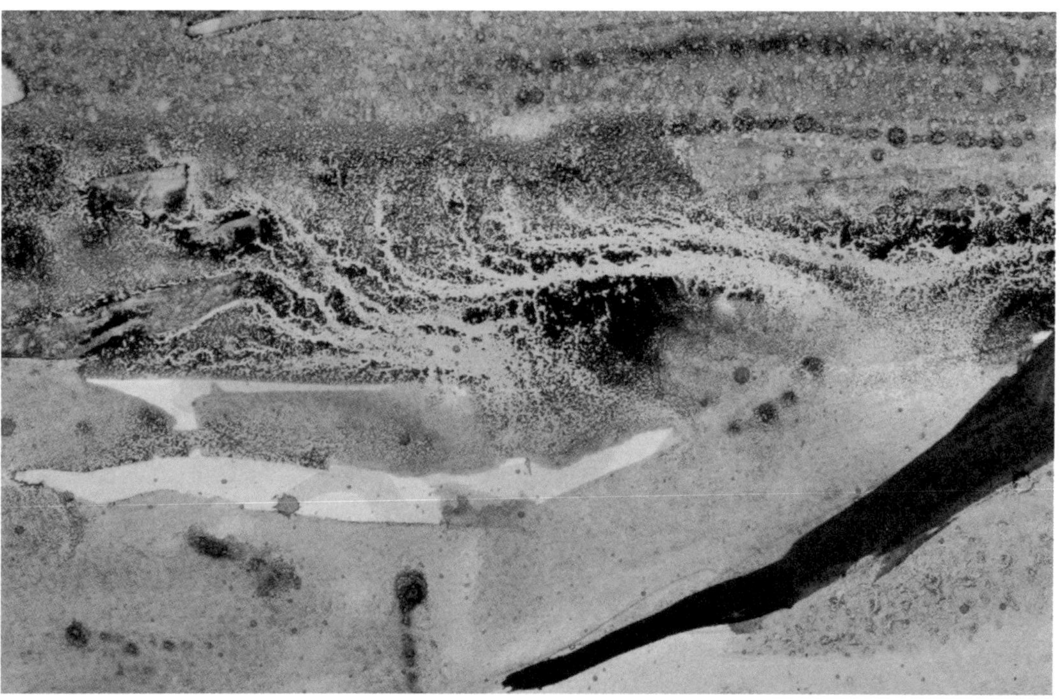

Detail of **Breaker**, 2023 (pp. 54–55)
Ink, sea salt and Eastbourne sea water
on paper, 153 × 342 cm
Showing ink dispersal due to sea water

be seen when you look closely at the drawing. I enjoy this materiality in drawing; the unexpected ways in which media and subject interact.

Alongside your polar work, the East Sussex coastline is a focus for this show. You've made frequent visits here and been thorough in your research of the area. How has this informed your work?
I want to connect audiences with familiar landscapes that are undergoing change due to rising sea levels. The iconic and recognisable coastline on Towner's doorstep is testament to these changes. Over the duration of my research, I've witnessed how the chalk cliffs are constantly being eroded with rock falls and beach closures. The historic National Trust café at Birling Gap is currently being dismantled due to the dangers of cliff erosion,[4] and the steps down to the sea that I depicted in my drawing *Hope Gap* (2022; p. 69) are currently closed because the sea is undermining their foundations and making them unstable.

As well as looking at scientific data that shows us the current and predicted rates of land erosion,[5] I've also walked extensively, recording landmarks such as Beachy Head (pp. 66 and 70–71) and Birling Gap, and observing cliff erosion at first hand. The extraordinary light that radiates off the sheer chalk cliffs is compelling and beautiful, but their scale is terrifying. It's a landscape that I'm wary of but one I've also become really attached to, and I wanted to try and capture this through my work.

Part of your research involved looking at historic works in the Towner collection that represent the East Sussex coastline, so that you could respond to these by drawing the corresponding viewpoints today. The comparisons clearly show the physical changes to this landscape. What did you learn through this process?
Some fascinating topographical drawings in the Towner collection show the coastline around Beachy Head and Birling Gap at the turn of the twentieth century. Elizabeth Smith Paget (1839–1931) was a regular visitor to

Eastbourne over a forty-year period. In revisiting some of the locations in which she drew, I tried to position myself in the same viewpoint to make a present-day comparative drawing. It soon became apparent that this would be impossible: most of her drawings were made from near the cliff edge and those sections of the cliff are now in the sea. In some cases, I had to rely on a drone to capture the exact position she drew from as the viewpoint is now metres out to sea.

Similarly, I have been looking at historic postcard views of the coastline taken over the last century. These too reveal large losses of coastline. A look at a 1960s postcard of Birling Gap coastguard cottages clearly shows the eight terraced houses. A present-day view shows that only four now remain, the rest having been demolished before they fell into the sea. Surveys made along Birling Gap between 1951 and 2013 clearly chart significant losses of the coastline. Sea erosion and extreme weather events have led to dramatic cliff erosion, with terraced cottages, boathouses and a café lost over the sixty-year period.

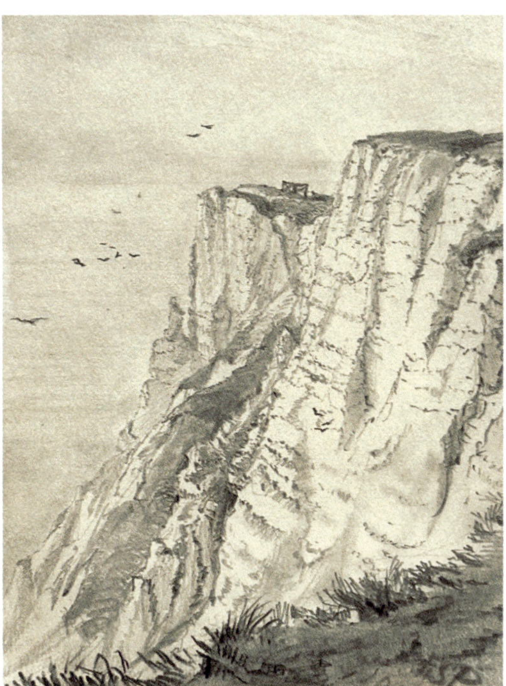

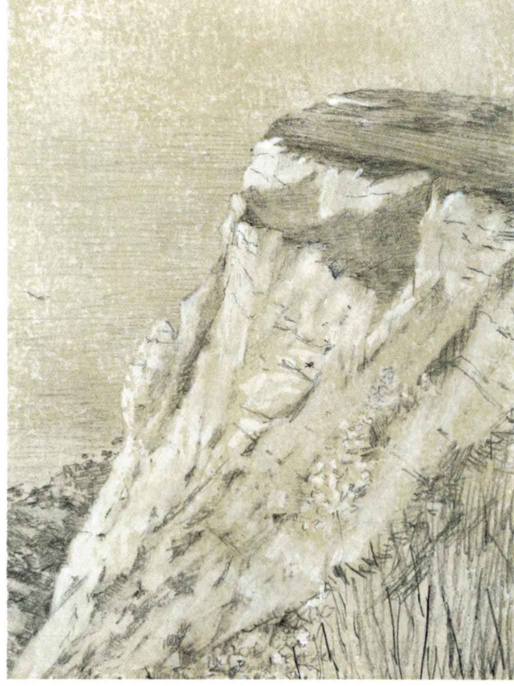

Left: Elizabeth Smith Paget
Cliffs at Beachy Head (detail), *c.* 1898
Pencil, pen and watercolour wash on paper,
17.7 × 12.6 cm
Towner Eastbourne

Right: Emma Stibbon
Cliffs at Beachy Head, 2024
Pencil, pen and watercolour wash on paper,
17.7 × 12.6 cm

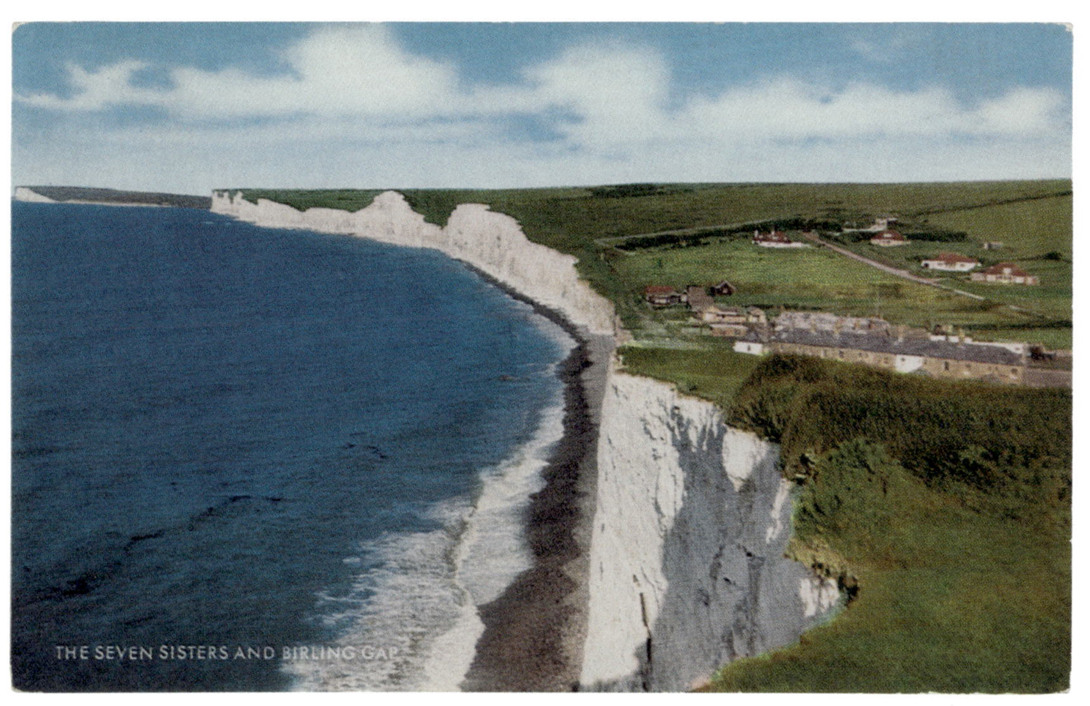

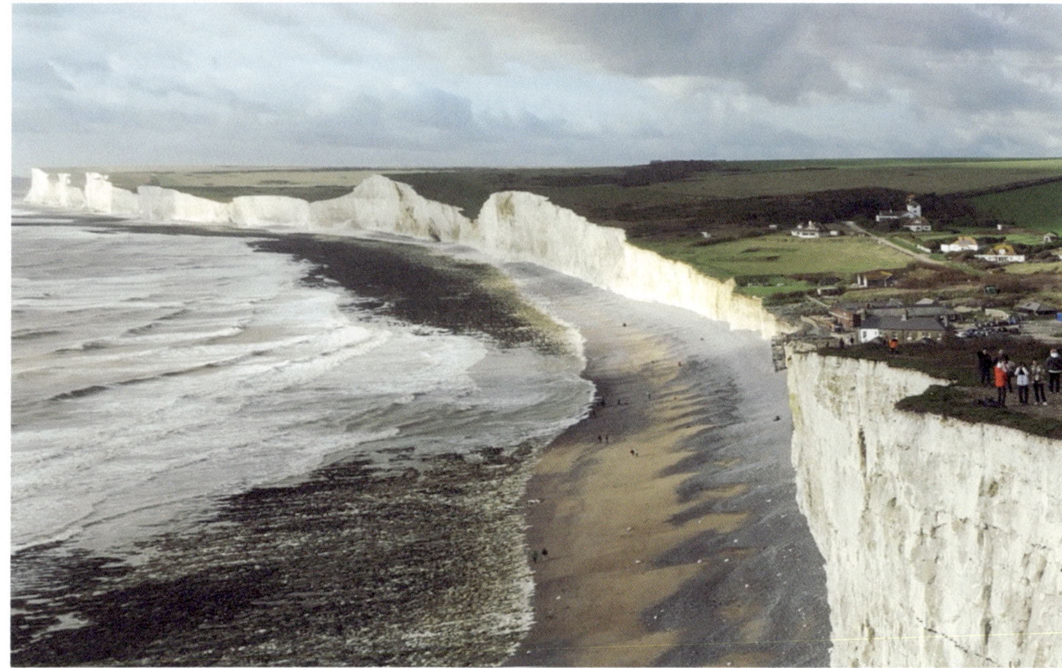

Top: J. Salmon Ltd
The Seven Sisters and Birling Gap,
31 October 1966
Postcard, 8.5 × 14 cm

Bottom: Emma Stibbon and Racquet Studios
The Seven Sisters and Birling Gap,
19 February 2024
8.5 x 14 cm
The white cottage at the left end of the
terrace is the central white cottage shown
in the postcard above

You typically make your drawings on paper.
Cliff Fall (2023), *the large-scale wall
installation and centrepiece of the Towner
exhibition, is fundamentally a drawing, but
what was your aim in moving away from
drawing on paper and into 3D installation
for this work?*
Standing under the precarious chalk cliffs
makes you feel very vulnerable. I wanted
to give a physical sense of the immensity of
them towering above, so I decided to make
an installation of a rock fall that projects out
of the wall and spills into the gallery space.
Working on such a large scale was like
creating a stage set, my aim being to create
the experience of being immersed in the
drawing. I made *Cliff Fall* to be installed
opposite *Breaker* in the gallery to suggest
the erosive power of the sea that pounds
the base of the cliffs, with the viewer trapped
between them.

*We've talked about how the exhibition
is not only a stark reminder of the impacts
of climate change but also, through the
beauty of your work, a way for audiences
both to appreciate what there is to lose
and to visualise some of the more distant
landscapes you've visited. Was this your
purpose?*
My primary motivations for making work
are awe and a fascination with the power
and beauty of nature. But I'm increasingly
conscious that we're living through
unprecedented times and as an artist I now
feel committed to recording my observations
of the impact of climate change in my work.

*We started our conversation thinking about
how changes in seemingly remote parts of
the globe affect our own familiar landscapes.
Of course, this implies the opposite, that
our behaviour affects other parts of the world.*
Indeed, although the UK is experiencing the
impact of rising sea levels and increased storm
events, other parts of the planet are seeing far
more destruction: the least carbon-emitting
societies are hit hardest and are the least
well equipped to deal with the consequences.
Our relationship with the landscape is very
uncertain, and we need to realise our
interconnectedness and our responsibilities
to other parts of the world. The question
is how we might adapt and to what degree
we can influence the future?

*What do you think art can offer people in
this context that perhaps science and politics
cannot?*
Increasingly I believe art has an important
role to play in the urgent debates of our time.
As an artist I feel I'm a witness to what is
happening in my lifetime, and the challenge
for me is how to render it through my
drawings. There is a tenderness to the human
touch of drawing that really connects us, it
has a directness that speaks in ways that hard
science can't. Although scientific data clearly
demonstrate the impact of dramatic increases
in global warming, and we can see the effects
of this for ourselves, perhaps the artist's more
creative methods of communication can
engage our emotions to provoke thought
and even help to galvanise us into changing
our behaviour.

Making **Cliff Fall**, 2023
Acrylic on gesso-prepared board
with chalk rocks and mixed media,
500 × 781.4 × 800 cm

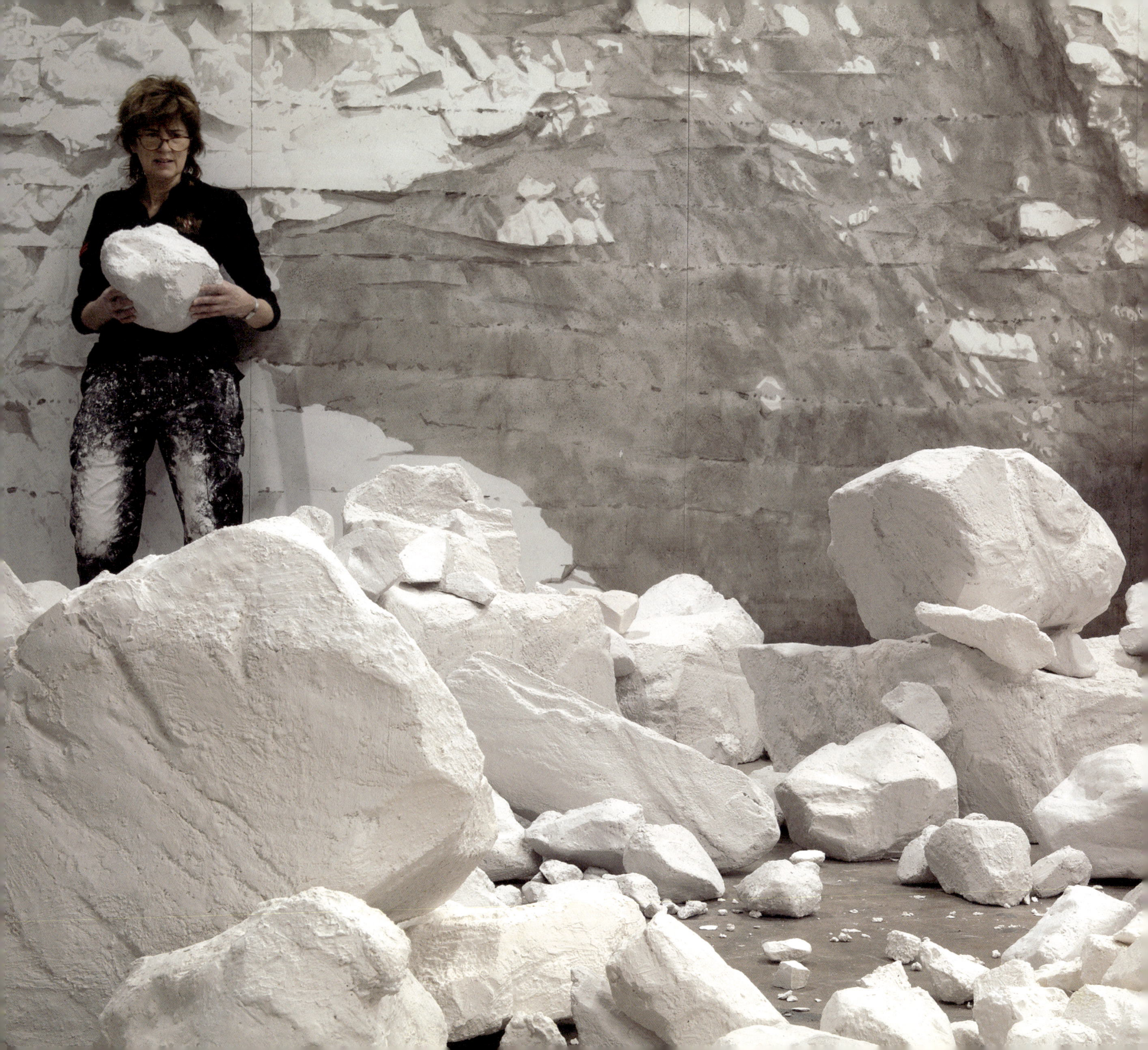

THE SUBLIMITY OF BOUNDLESS LANDSCAPES

Richard Fisher

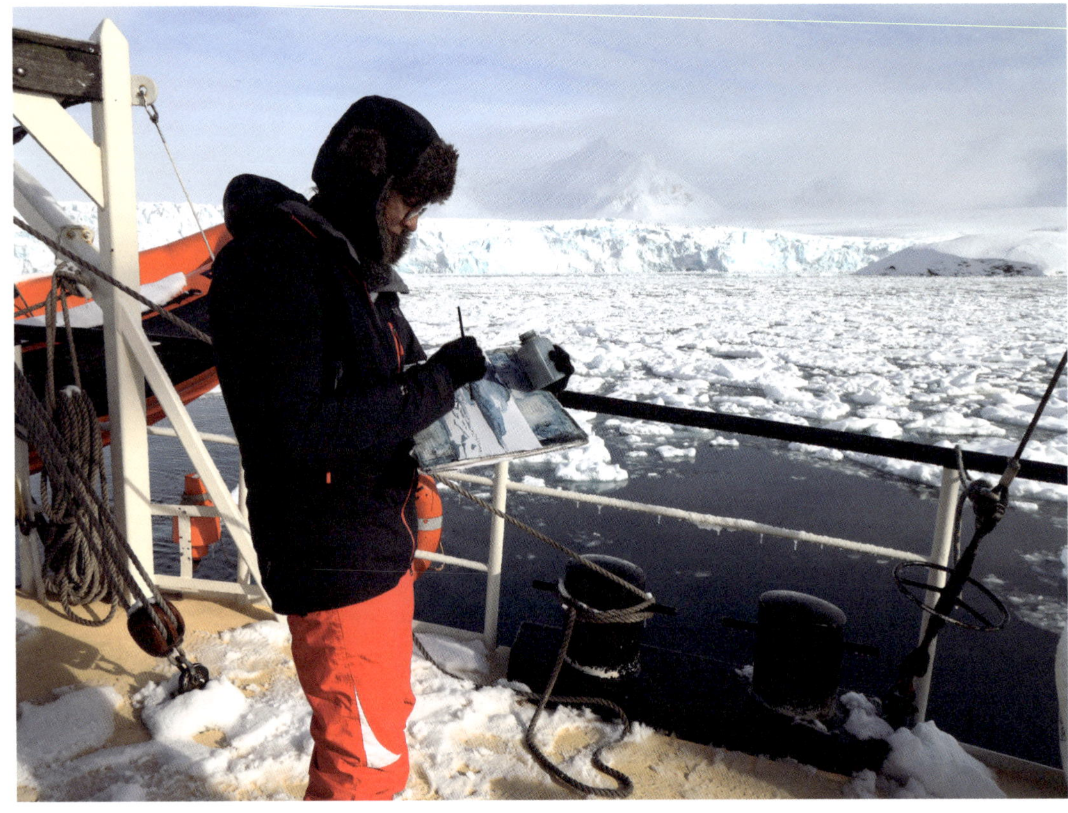

In his influential treatise on the sublime, first published in 1757, Edmund Burke described the overwhelming effect of encountering boundlessness. 'The ideas of eternity, and infinity, are among the most affecting we have,' he wrote. 'Infinity has a tendency to fill the mind with that sort of delightful horror, which is the most genuine effect, and truest test of the sublime.'[1] Not many things are truly infinite, he continued, but when you struggle to see a boundary or edge, they can feel as though they are. 'The imagination meets no check which may hinder its extending them at pleasure,' Burke wrote. Such encounters may take place far afield – the experience of gazing across Antarctica's seemingly endless ice sheets, for example – but they can also occur within reach of everyday life, such as when we stand on the terrifyingly precipitous cliff at Beachy Head.

Burke and his contemporaries believed apparent boundlessness – as well as such other qualities as overwhelming power or mysterious obscurity – could provoke a unique mixture of awe and dread. This feeling, they proposed, could uplift the mind, enrich the soul and foster a clearer awareness of our relationship with the natural world. The philosopher Immanuel Kant called the sensation 'negative pleasure';[2] others used more colourful terms, such as 'terrible joy',[3] 'sweet shudder'[4] or 'rude kind of magnificence'.[5]

Emma Stibbon is no stranger to the sublime. Indeed, a few years ago she made a BBC Radio 3 documentary on the topic, following in the footsteps of J. M. W. Turner and other Grand Tourists in the Alps.[6] The immensity and power of nature – a boundless frozen vista, an erupting volcano, an obscure ocean – can be observed in much of her work. In 'Melting Ice | Rising Tides', she brings together sublime polar landscapes with moments from the unstable British coastline, as she explores how distant warming is having an impact closer to home. Sketches from her field trips to Antarctica and Svalbard in the High Arctic sit alongside works from the evolving south coast of England.

I was particularly struck by Burke's words on infinity when standing in front of Stibbon's two-metre-tall drawing *Hope Gap* (2022; p. 69), based on a beach and cliff-edge in East Sussex that is slowly being eaten away by the ocean. A series of steps descend beyond the surface of a roiling, rising sea. They seem as if they might continue downwards forever. The ocean, too, has no firm horizon or sharp coastline to provide us with a reassuring boundary. Sublime force is there as well: at the base of the steps, wave after wave strikes this impudently manmade structure as it clings to the land. As Burke wrote: 'I know of nothing sublime, which is not some modification of power.'[7] Indeed, the relentless force of the ocean at Hope Gap is now clear: in late 2023 the steps were closed to the public because their foundations had been undermined by the sea, making them unsafe.[8]

All along the British coastline, the ocean is eating away at cliffs and beaches, often taking houses, roads and other human constructions with it. As sea levels rise due to climate change, these losses are accelerating. In 'Melting Ice | Rising Tides', Stibbon seeks to connect this slow erosion with its distant origin: the anthropogenic heating of ice sheets many thousands of miles away. Combining the disintegration of UK cliffs and distant polar landscapes, her works help to close a geographical and climatological gap seemingly too immense and overwhelming for the mind to grapple with.

In Stibbon's landscapes, *temporal* magnitudes are also present. In her drawings of the creviced, disintegrating cliffs of England, which have the familiar strangeness of photographic negatives, she uses real chalk – a rock made of microscopic plankton that sank within a tropical sea many millions of years ago – to create parts of their compositions. It's a reminder that much of the land that we've dwelt and built upon has, after all, been underwater for millions of years – and from the rock's perspective, our human presence will be gone a mere moment after it arrived. If you blew on her chalk drawings, Stibbon tells me, the image would be lost; their compositions are as ephemeral as we are.

The thought of our own transience in deep time may seem a cold, distancing idea, but Stibbon's landscapes are rooted within human experience, even as the minutes, hours, years and eons pass. Signs of human life – like the steps at Hope Gap – may not always be present in her works, but the artist always is. You can see that presence in the details: strokes where her brush froze stiff in the cold, or drops of snow and sleet that fell onto the page. As clouds moved, waves rose and the wind blew, you can get a sense of the artist shivering out on the deck of a boat, trying to capture a fleeting moment in time. Much of Stibbon's work also contains materials from the places she records: as well as the chalk from England's cliffs, her glaciers contain ground rock flour collected from beneath the glacier ice, and the scene of Hope Gap contains sea salt mixed with the pigment.

Our world is changing fast as a result of climate change, so for the sake of future generations, we need to capture it – to *observe*. By now, the polar icebergs that Stibbon saw will long since have drifted away, and perhaps melted. In a warming world, more ice disappears every year. Meanwhile, British cliff edges continually retreat, giving rise to periodic, catastrophic collapses. Yesterday's coastline is not tomorrow's. In 'Melting Ice | Rising Tides', postcards of Birling Gap in East Sussex show landscapes that no longer exist. The vantage points in these can no longer be stood upon: the sea has taken the ground on which the photographer stood.

Through Stibbon's perspective, though, we can discover a deeper connection with and an understanding of these sublime transformations, as they happen. All her work is rooted in a place and a time – in being there, and bearing witness.

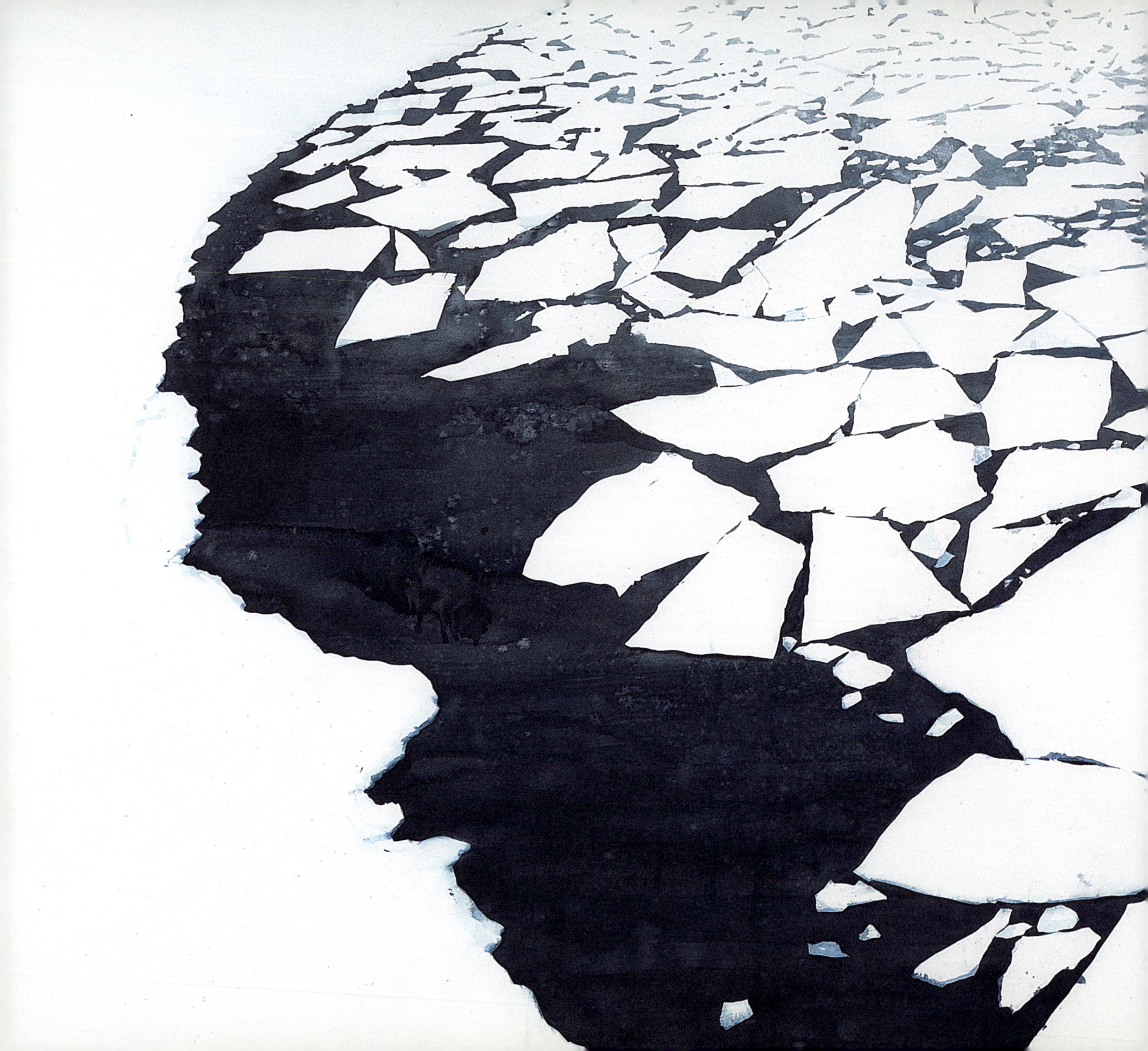

PLATES

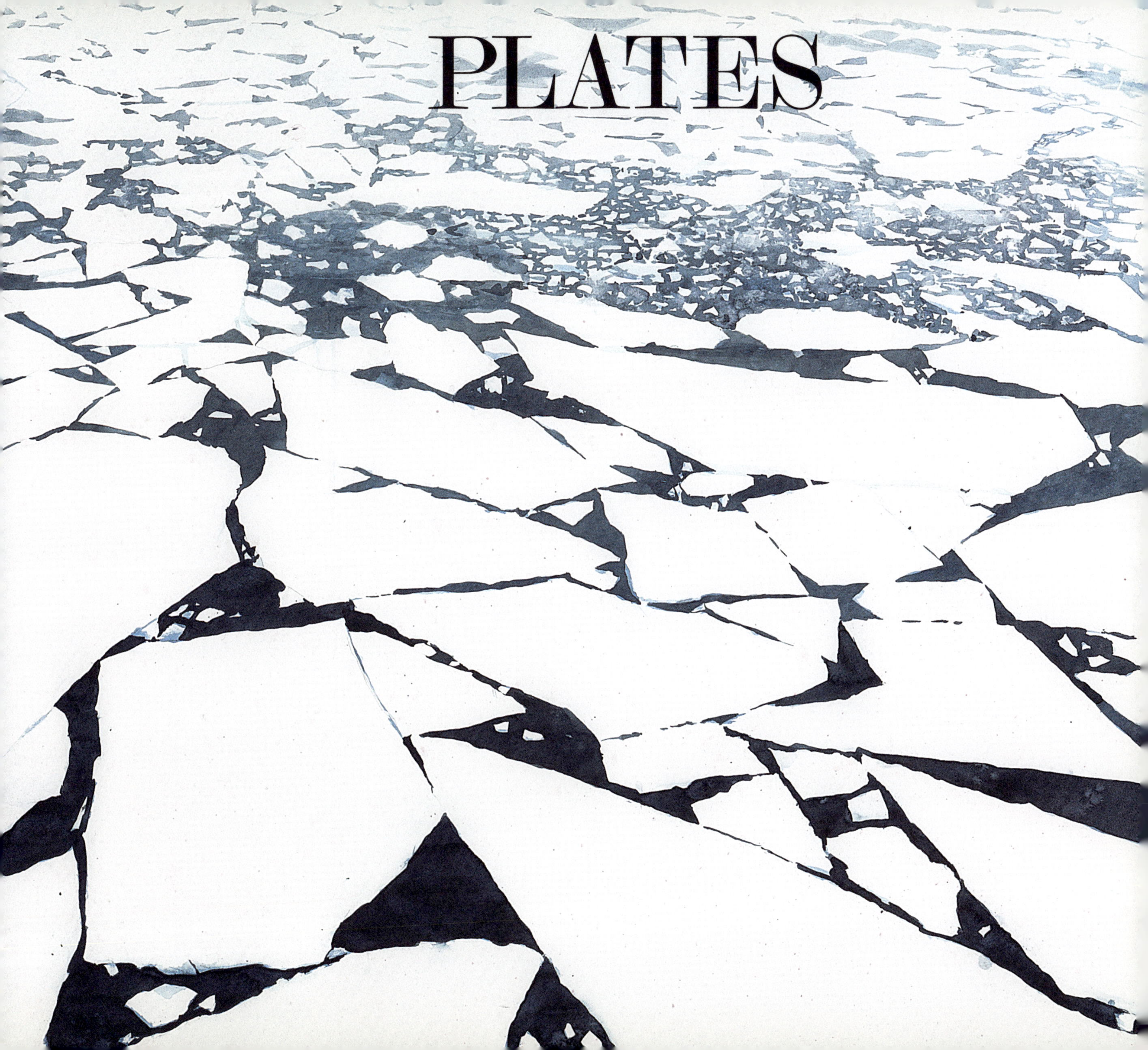

Berg I, 2023
Watercolour and graphite on paper, 122 × 179 cm

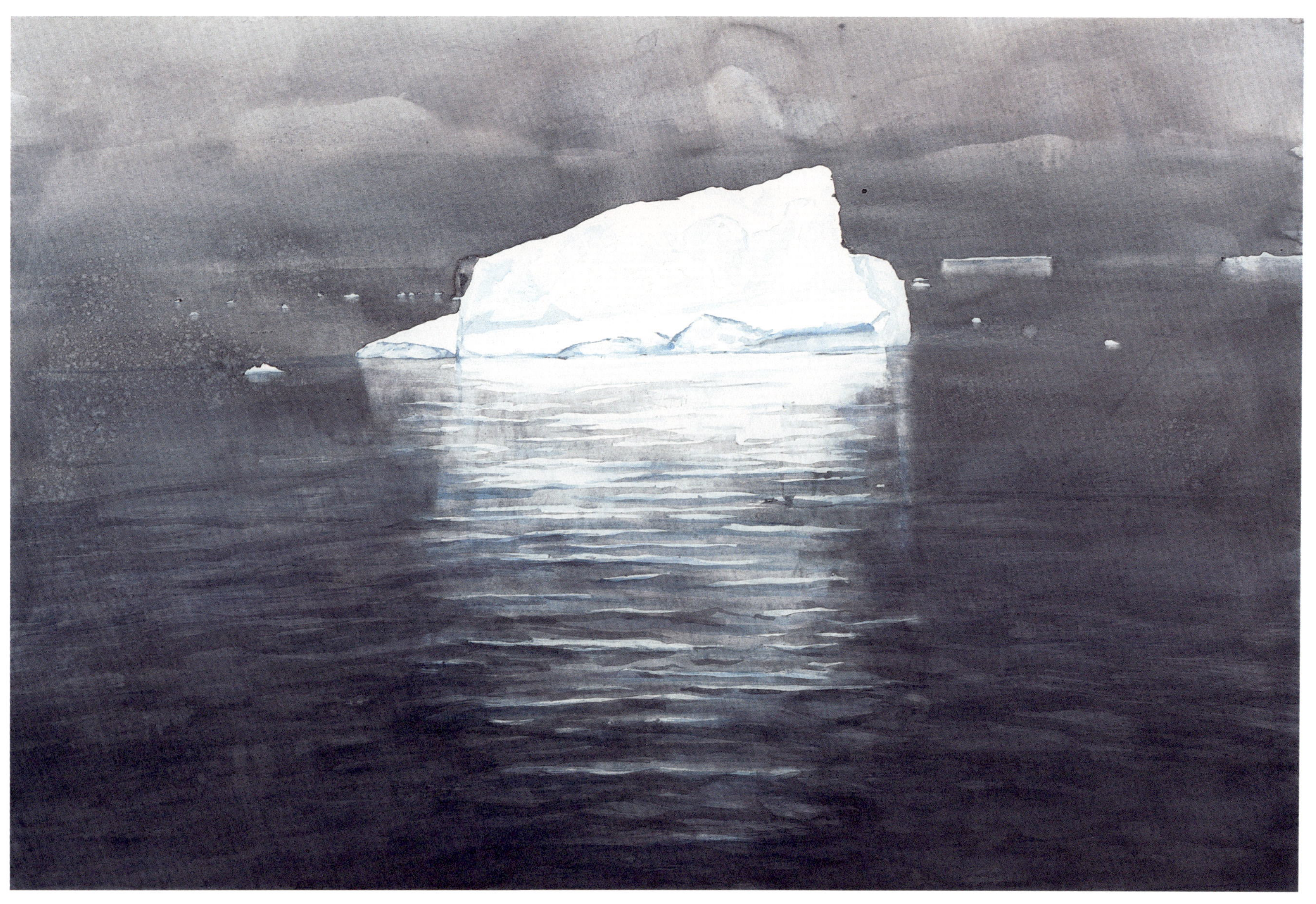

Berg II, 2023
Watercolour and graphite on paper, 122 × 180.5 cm

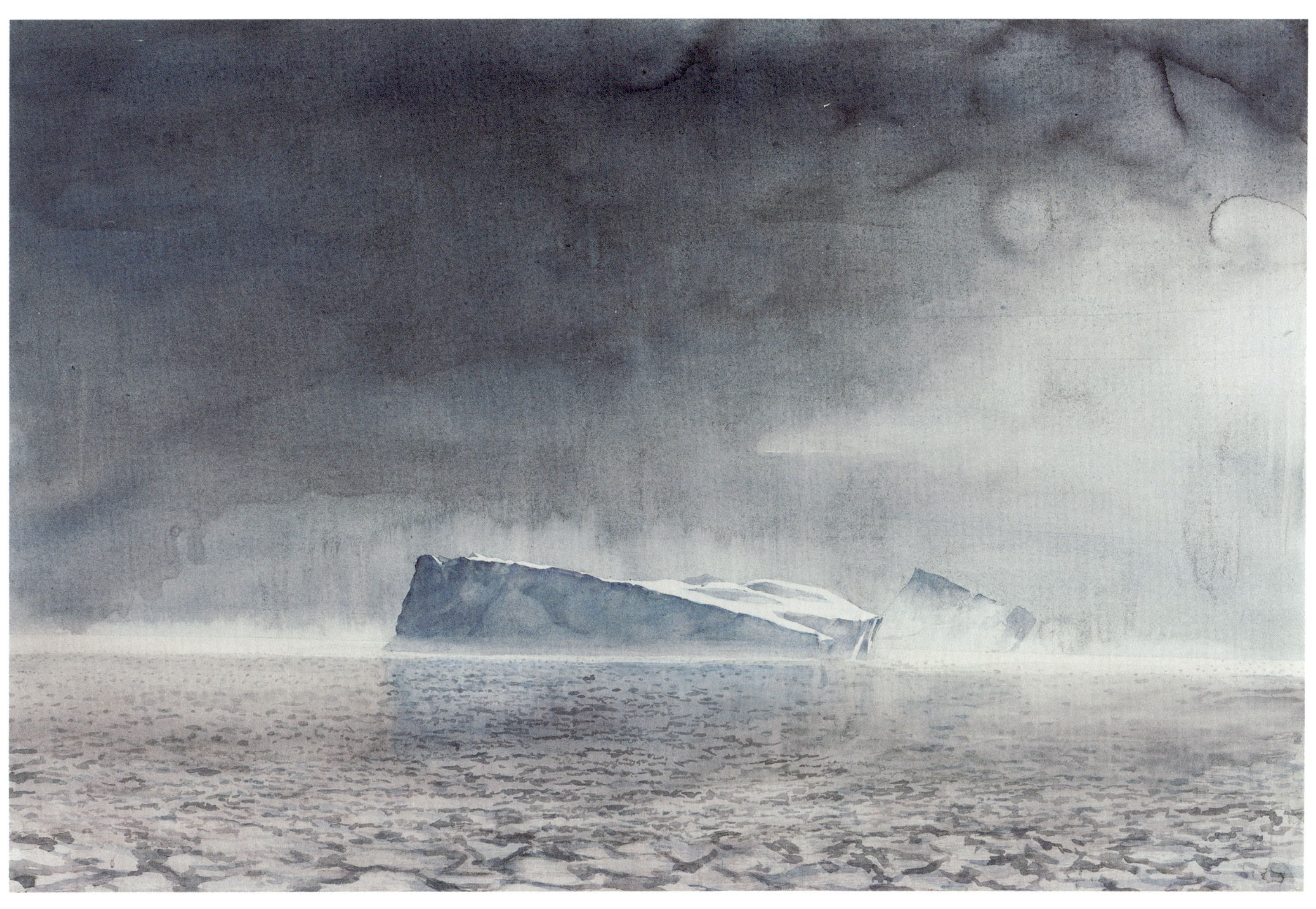

Berg III, 2023
Watercolour and graphite on paper, 123 × 178 cm

Overleaf
Detail of **Berg III**, 2023

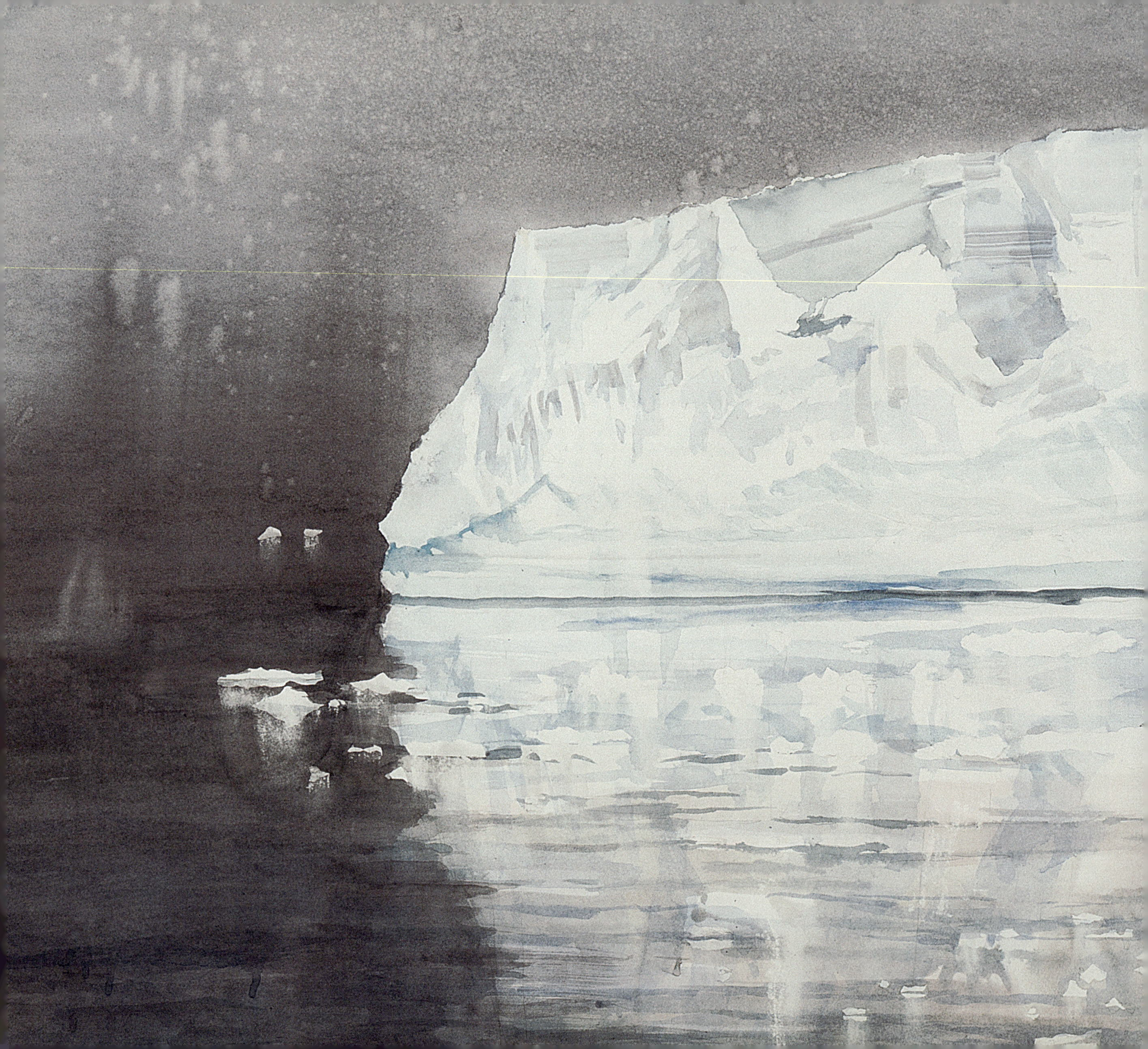

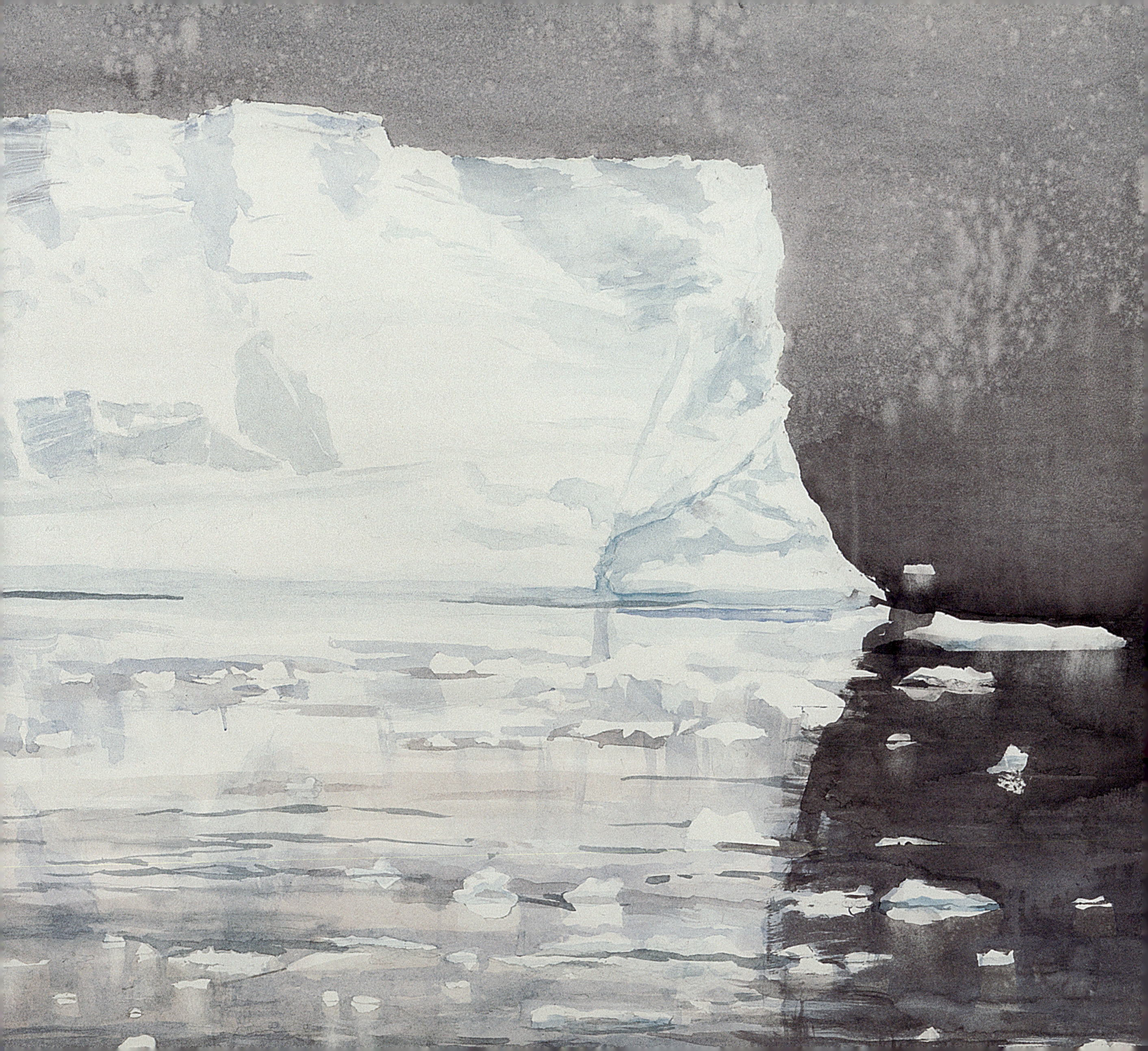

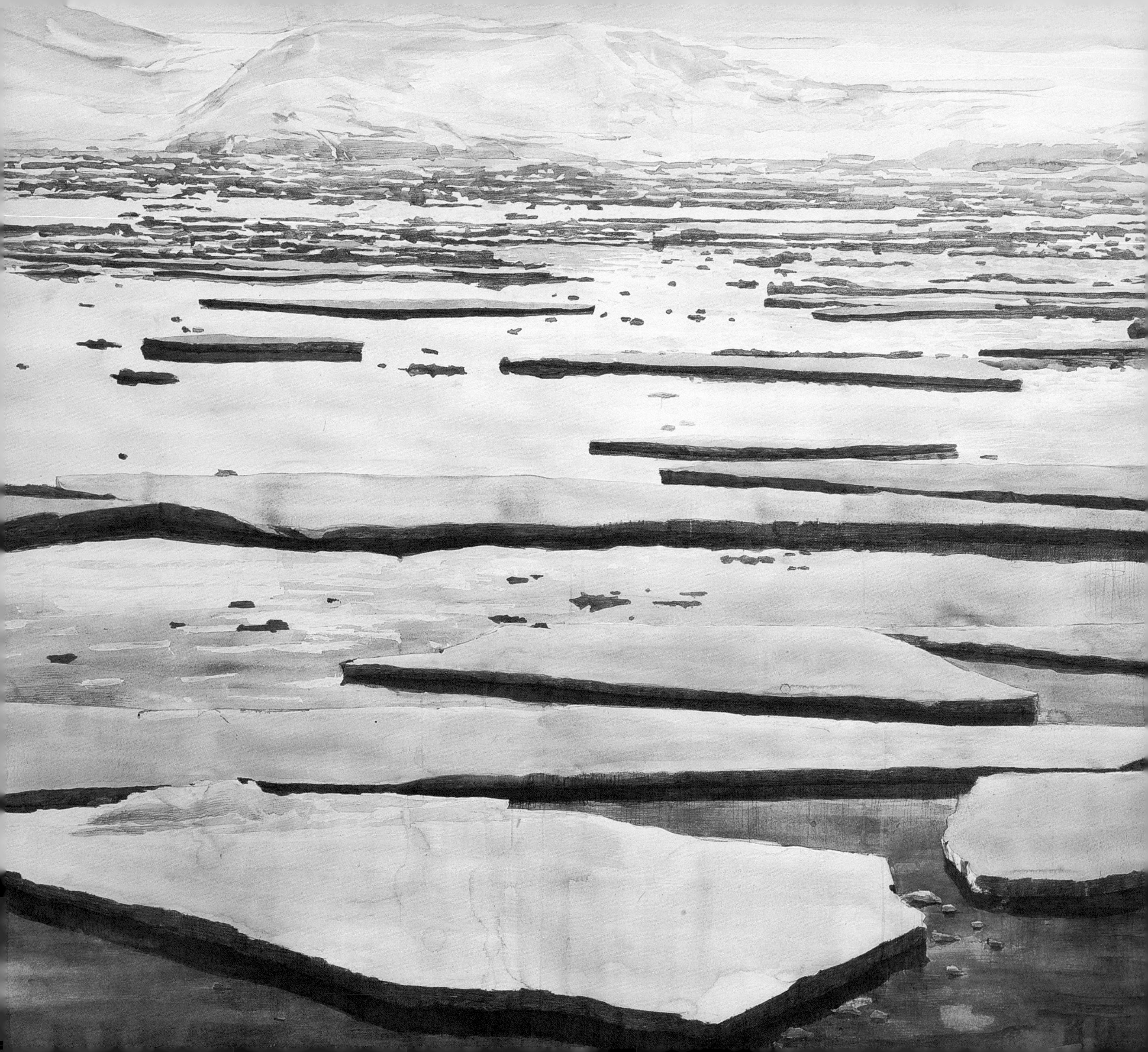

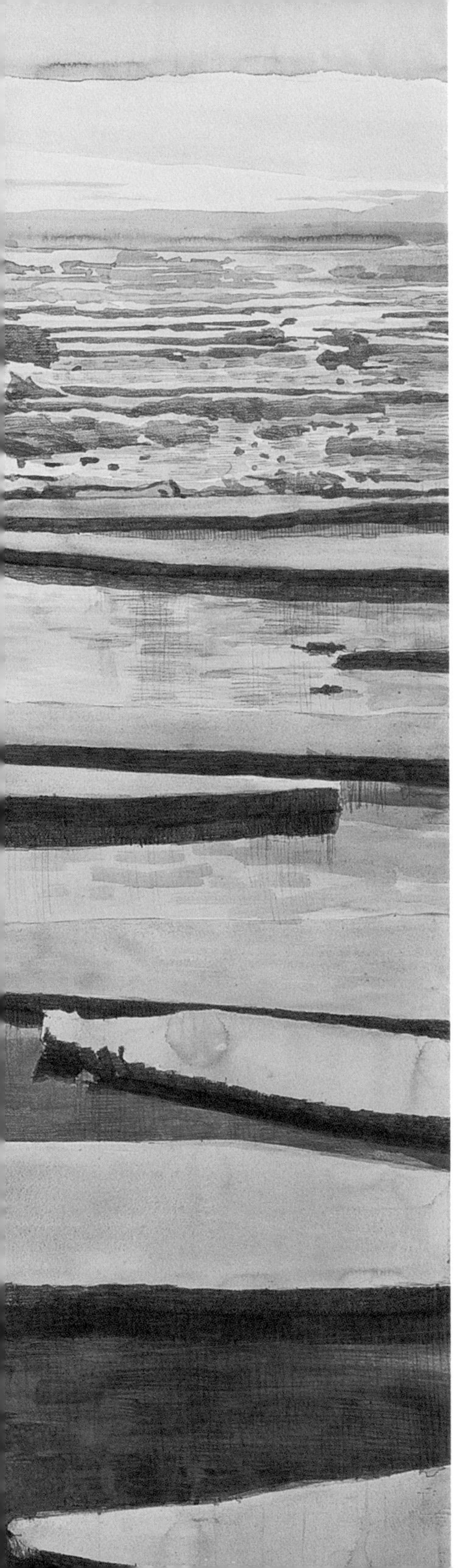

Drift Ice, 2014
Watercolour and graphite on paper,
153 × 213.5 cm

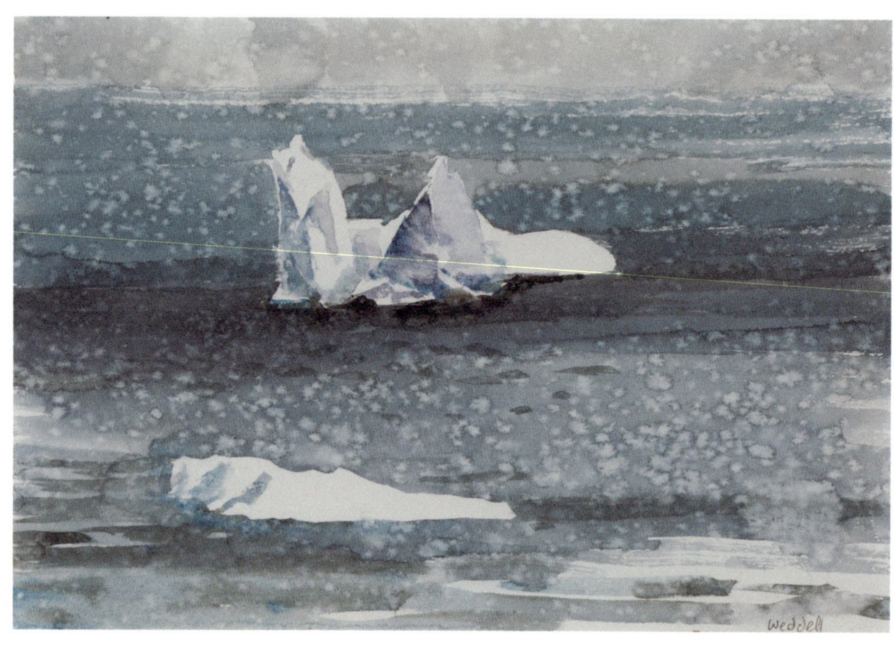

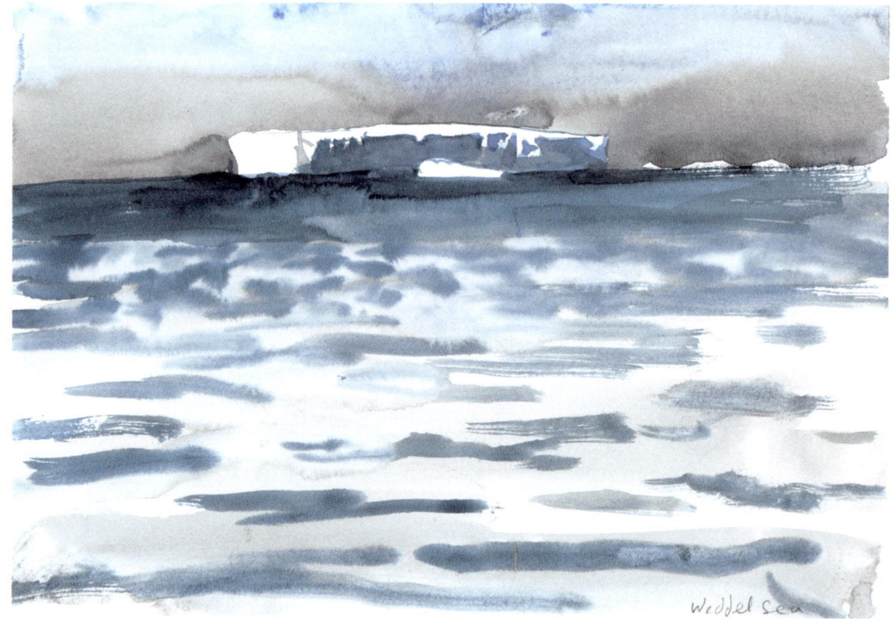

Weddell Sea, pages from Antarctica sketchbook, 2023
Watercolour on paper, each 21 × 29.7 cm

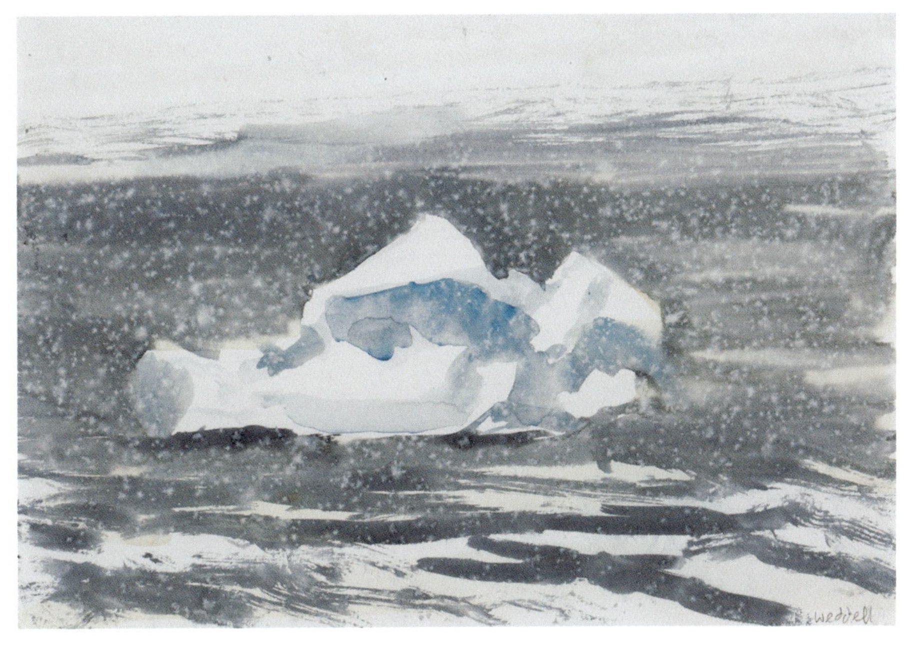

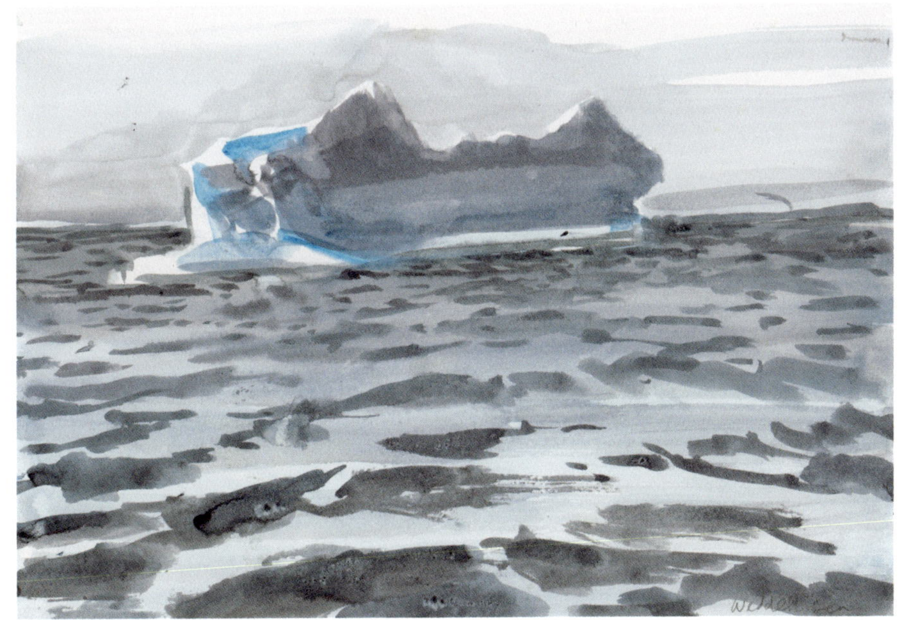

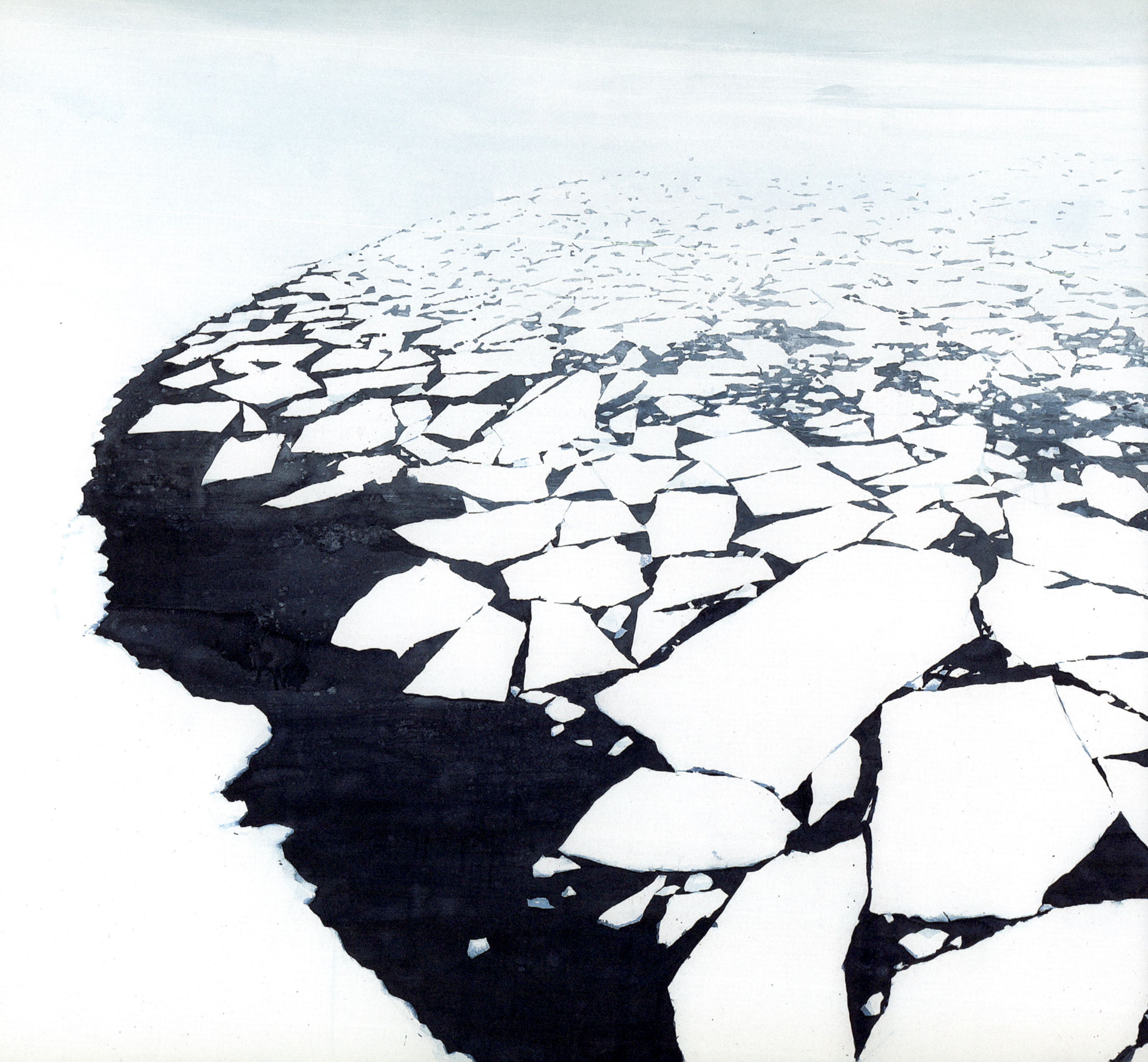

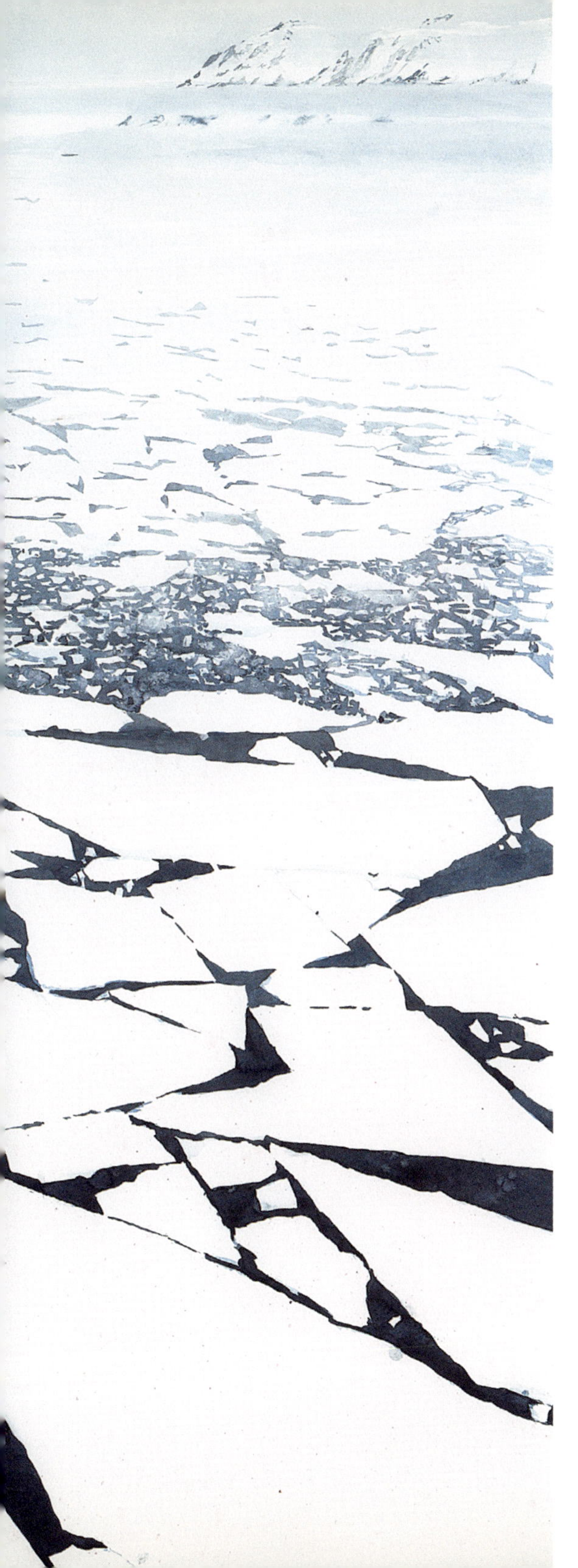

Sea Ice, Svalbard, 2023
Watercolour on paper, 153 × 224 cm

Ice Front I, 2020
Watercolour, graphite and aluminium
powder on paper, 153 × 185 cm

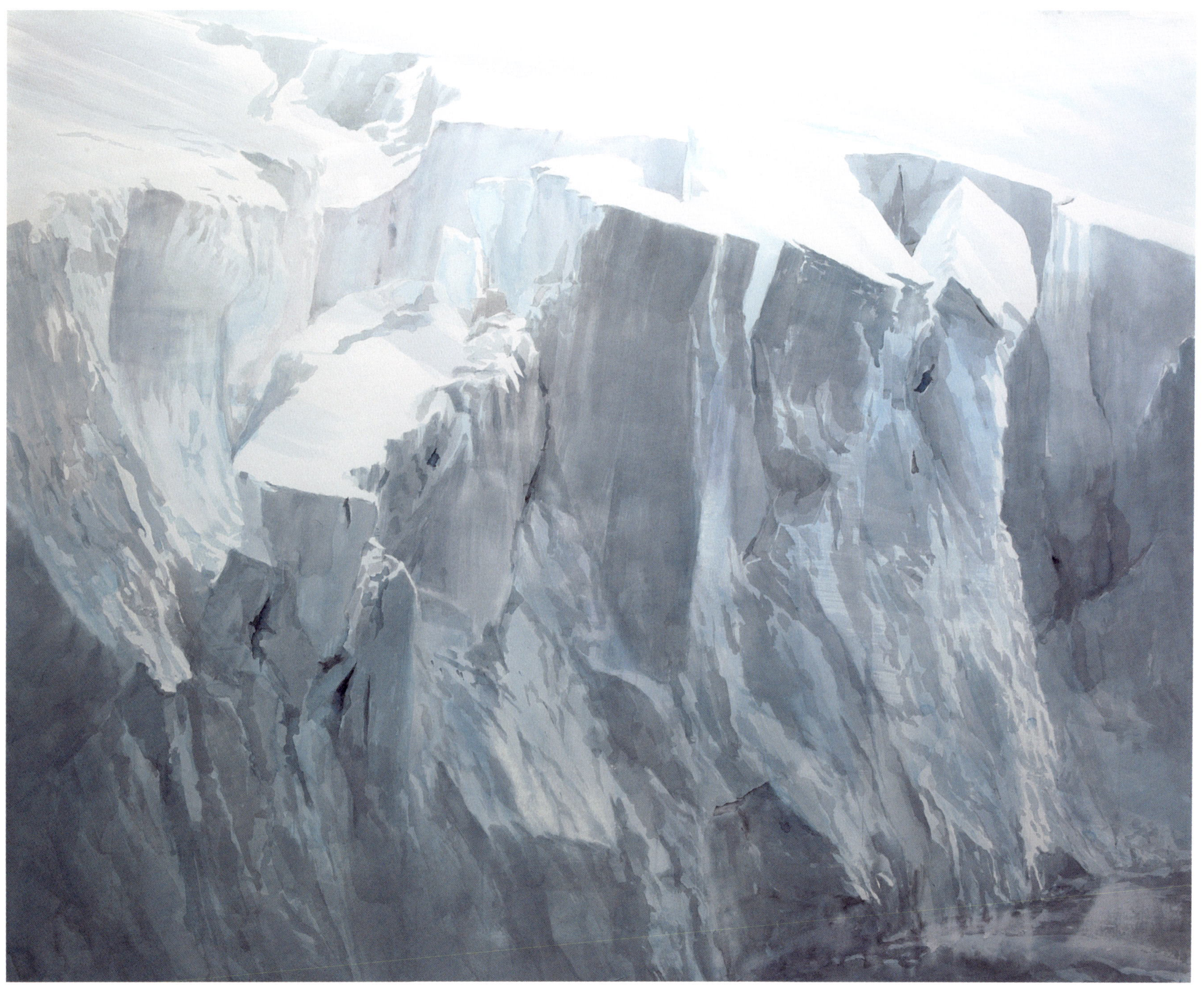

Ice Front II, 2020
Watercolour, graphite and aluminium
powder on paper, 153 × 185 cm

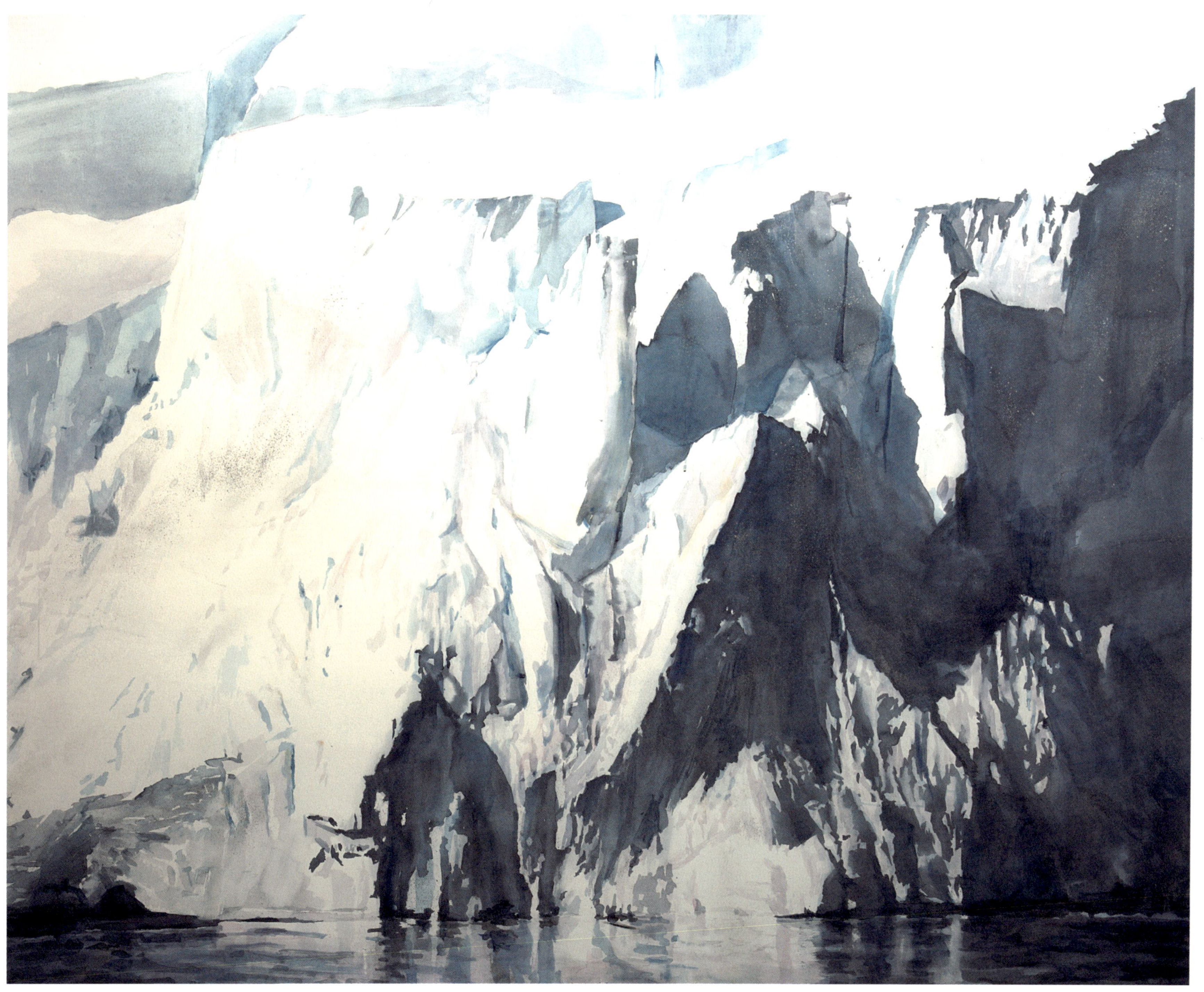

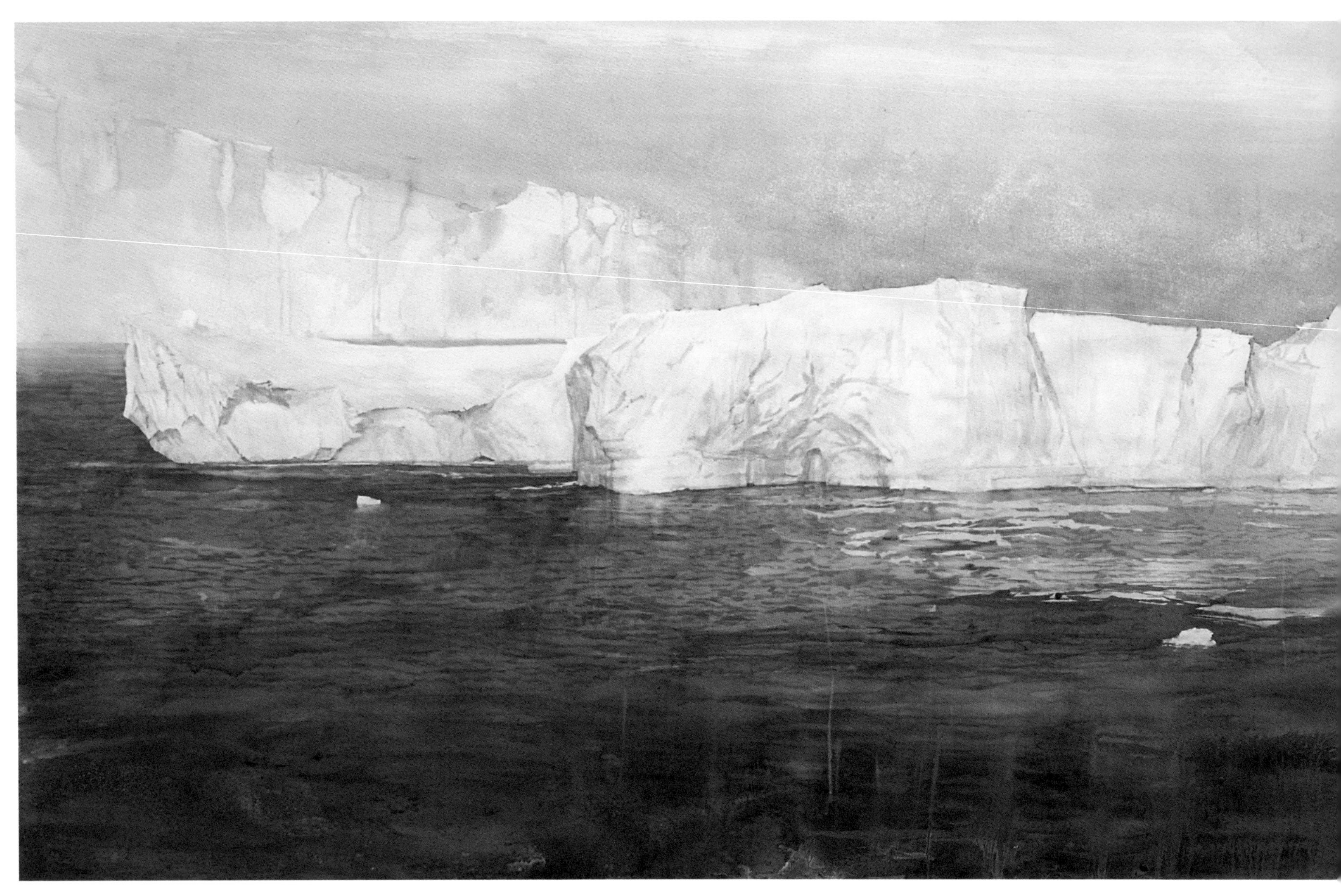

Tabular Berg, 2014
Watercolour, pigment and graphite
on paper, 150 × 350 cm
The Devonshire Collections, Chatsworth

Overleaf
Tabular Berg, 2022 (detail)
Intaglio print on paper, 48 × 75 cm

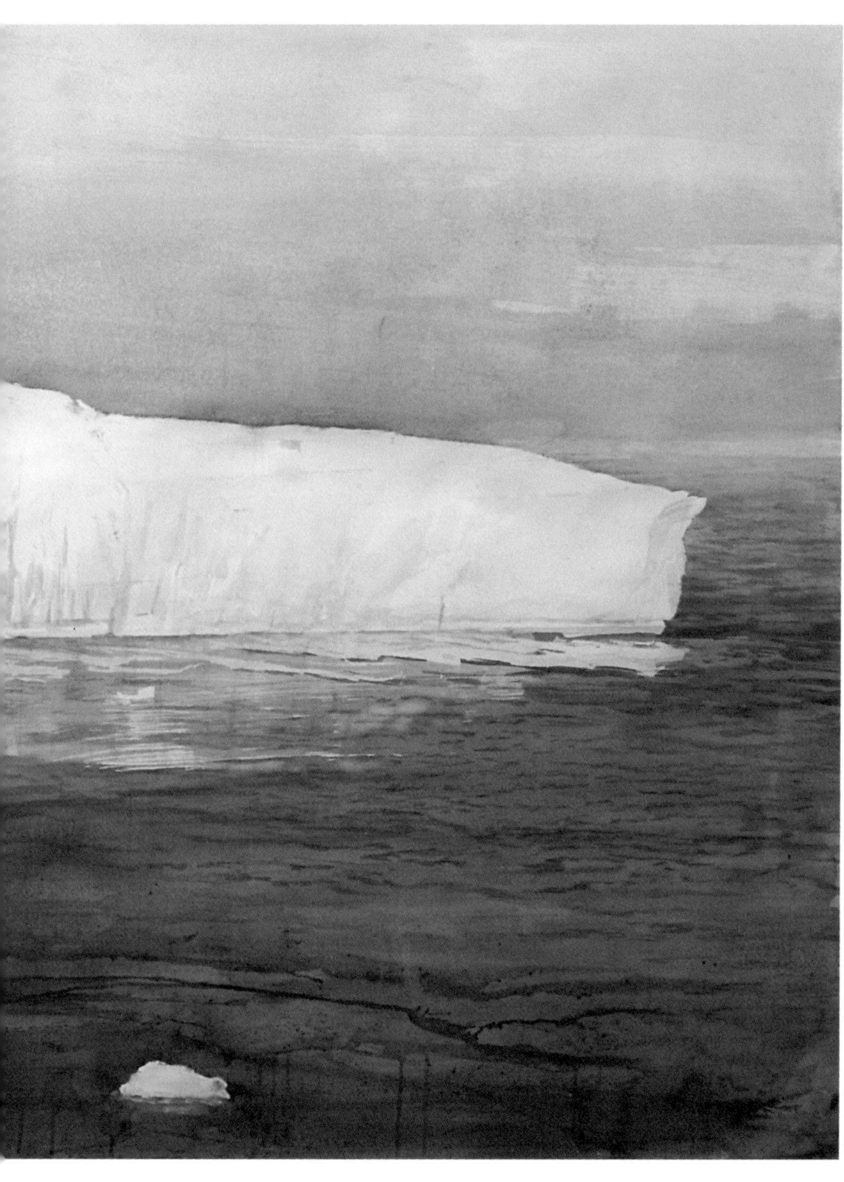

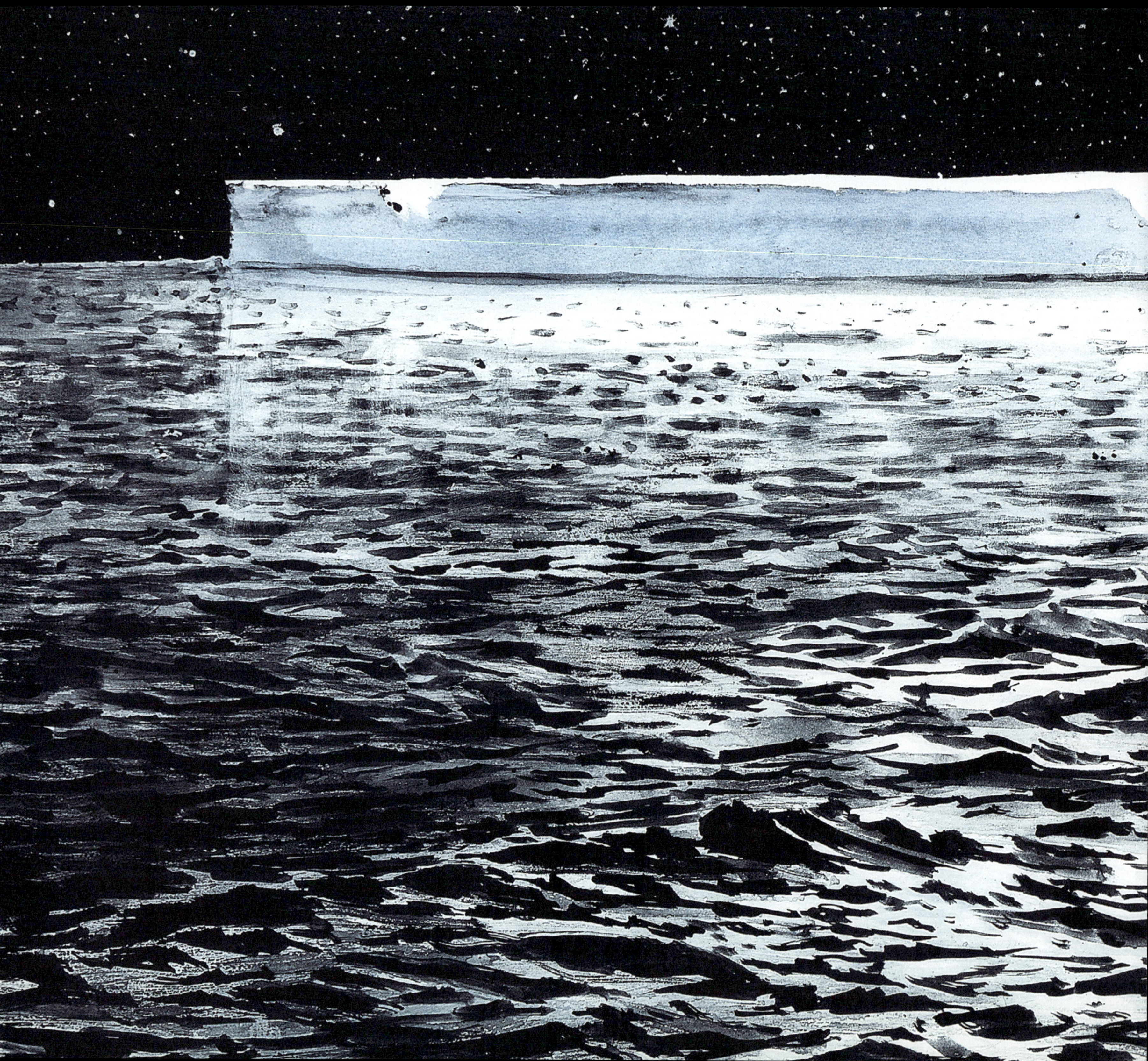

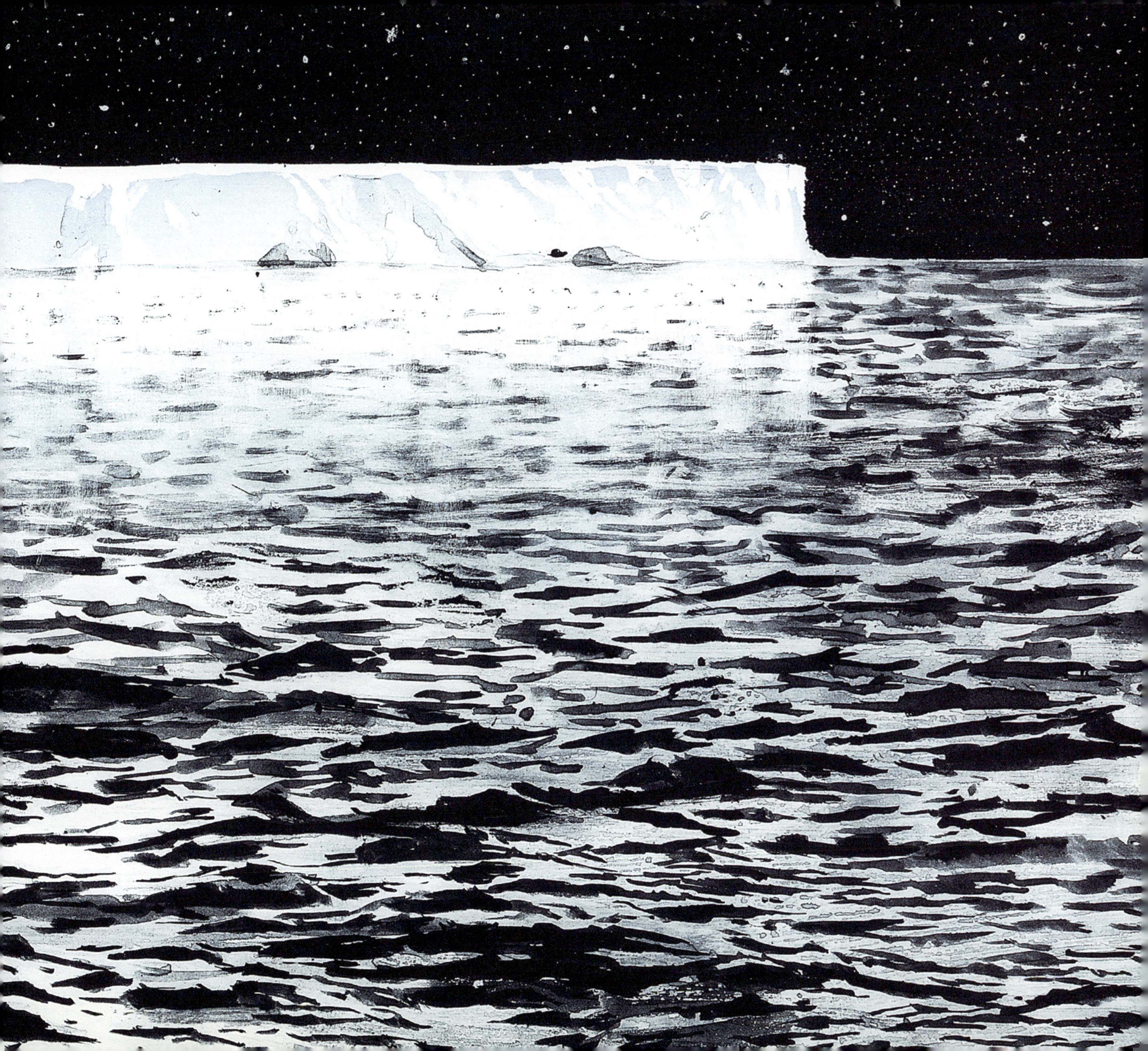

Berg Constellation, 2016
Intaglio print on paper, 26 × 36.5 cm

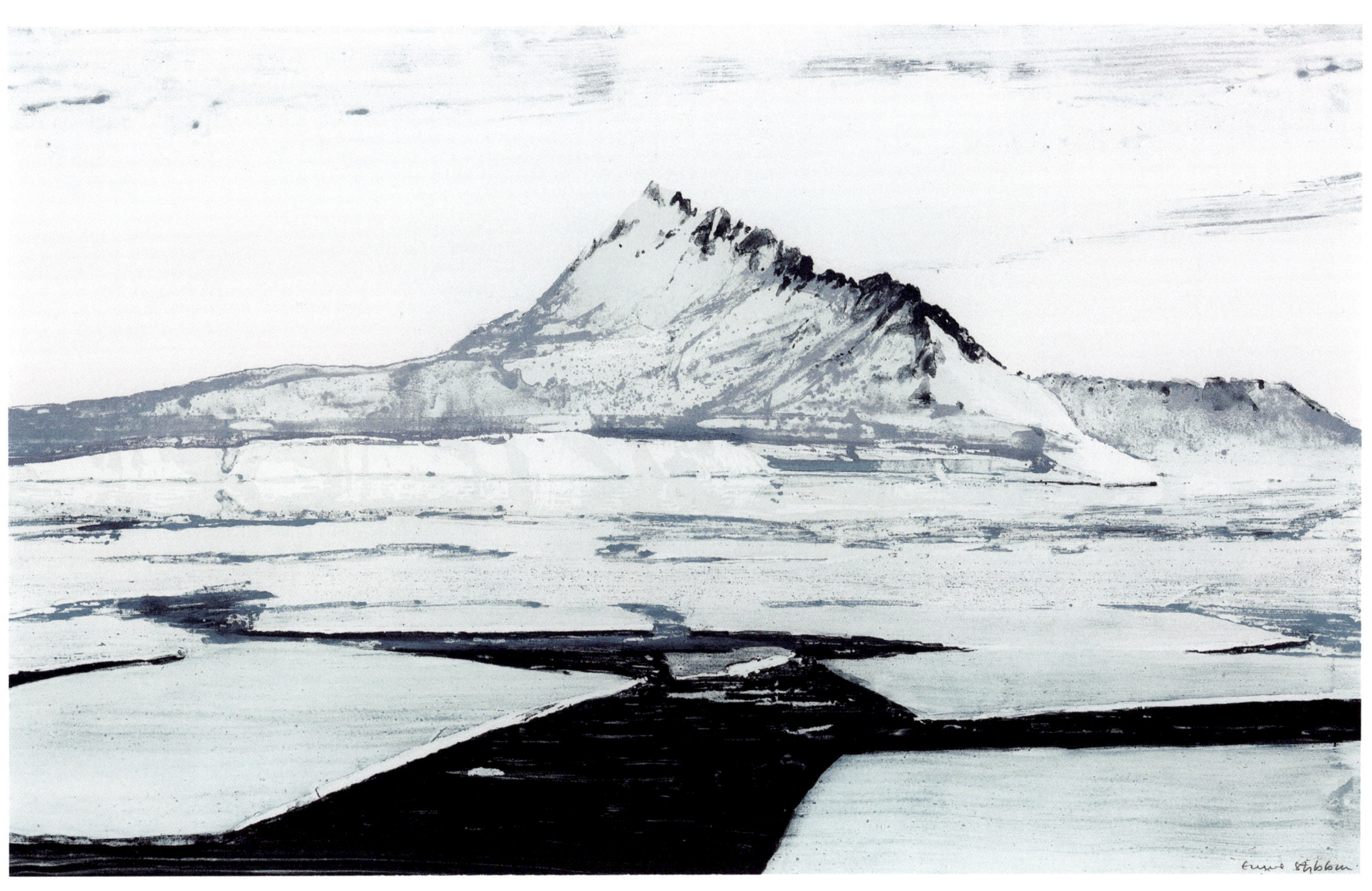

Ice Floe, Antarctica, 2020
Intaglio print with woodcut and hand
colouring on paper, 48 × 76 cm

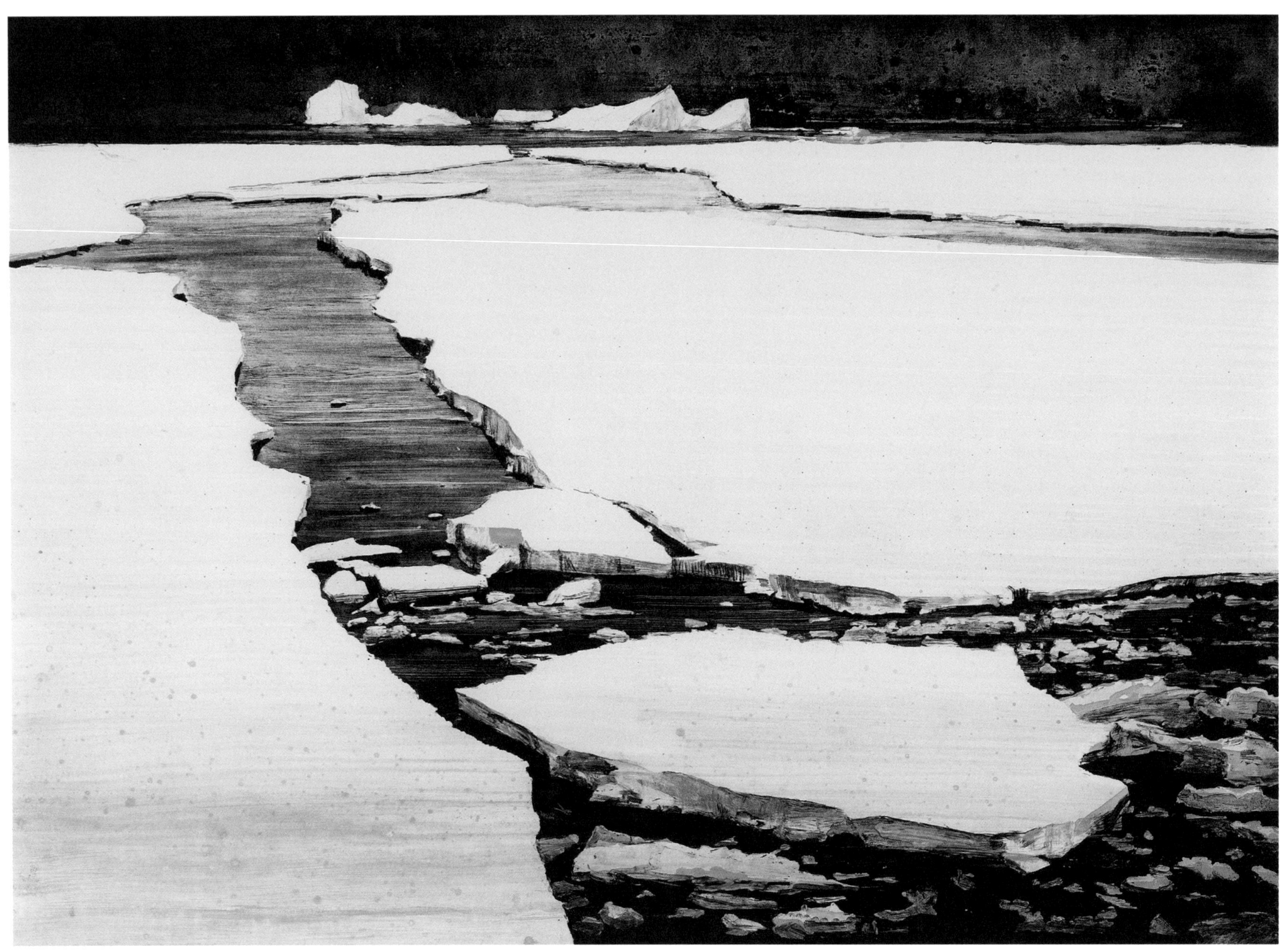

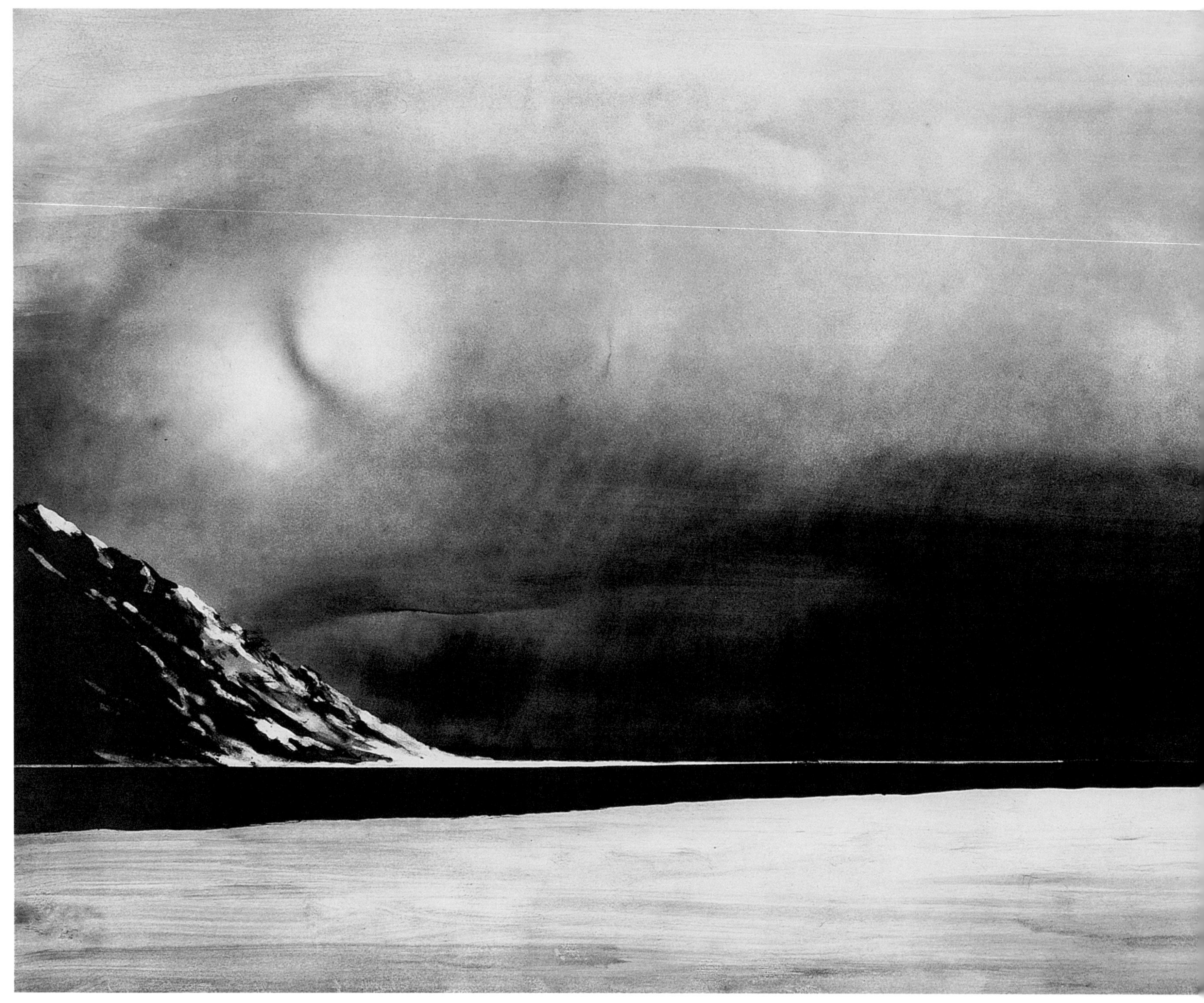

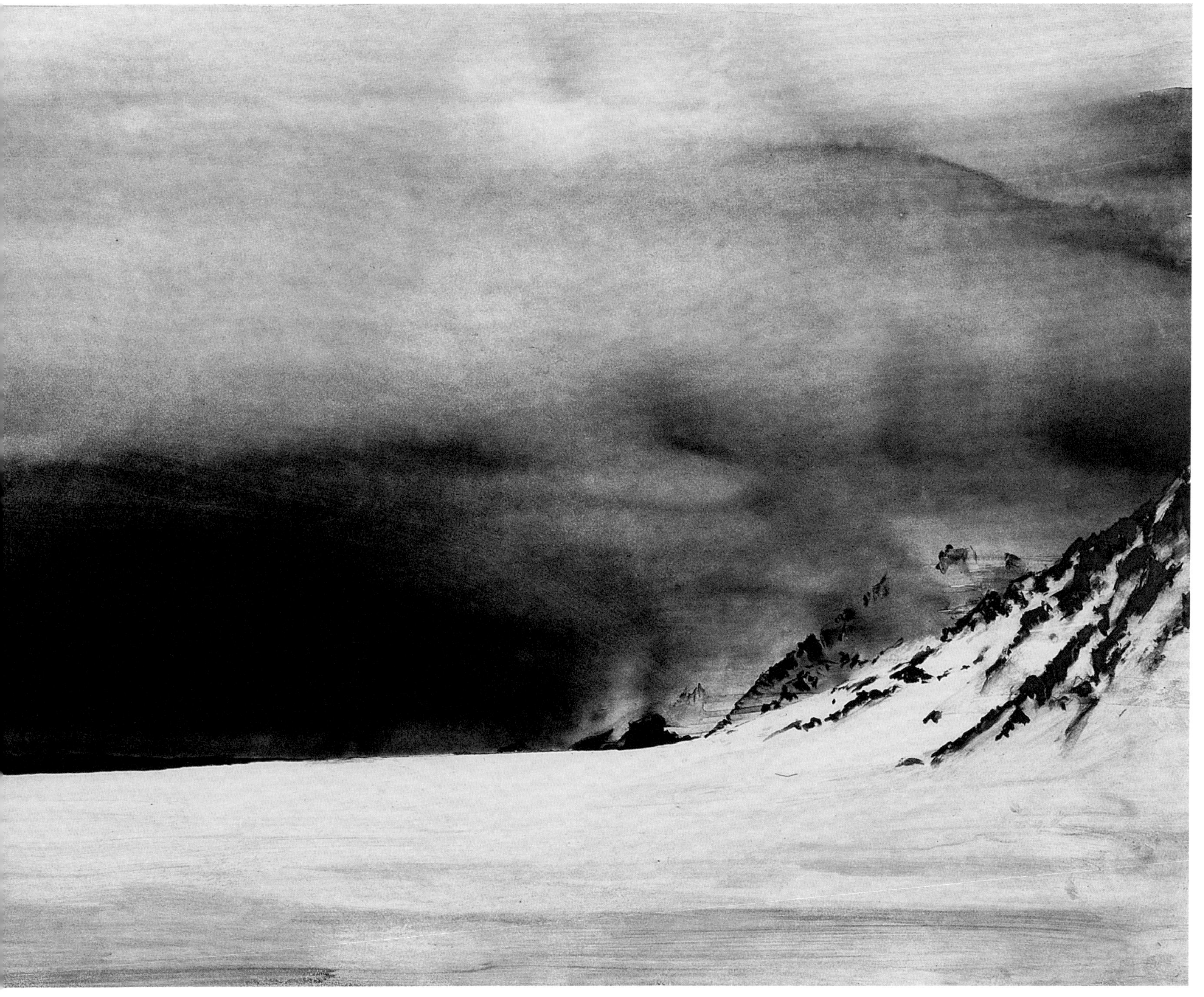

Ice Shelf, Svalbard, 2024
Intaglio print on paper, 47.5 × 70.7 cm

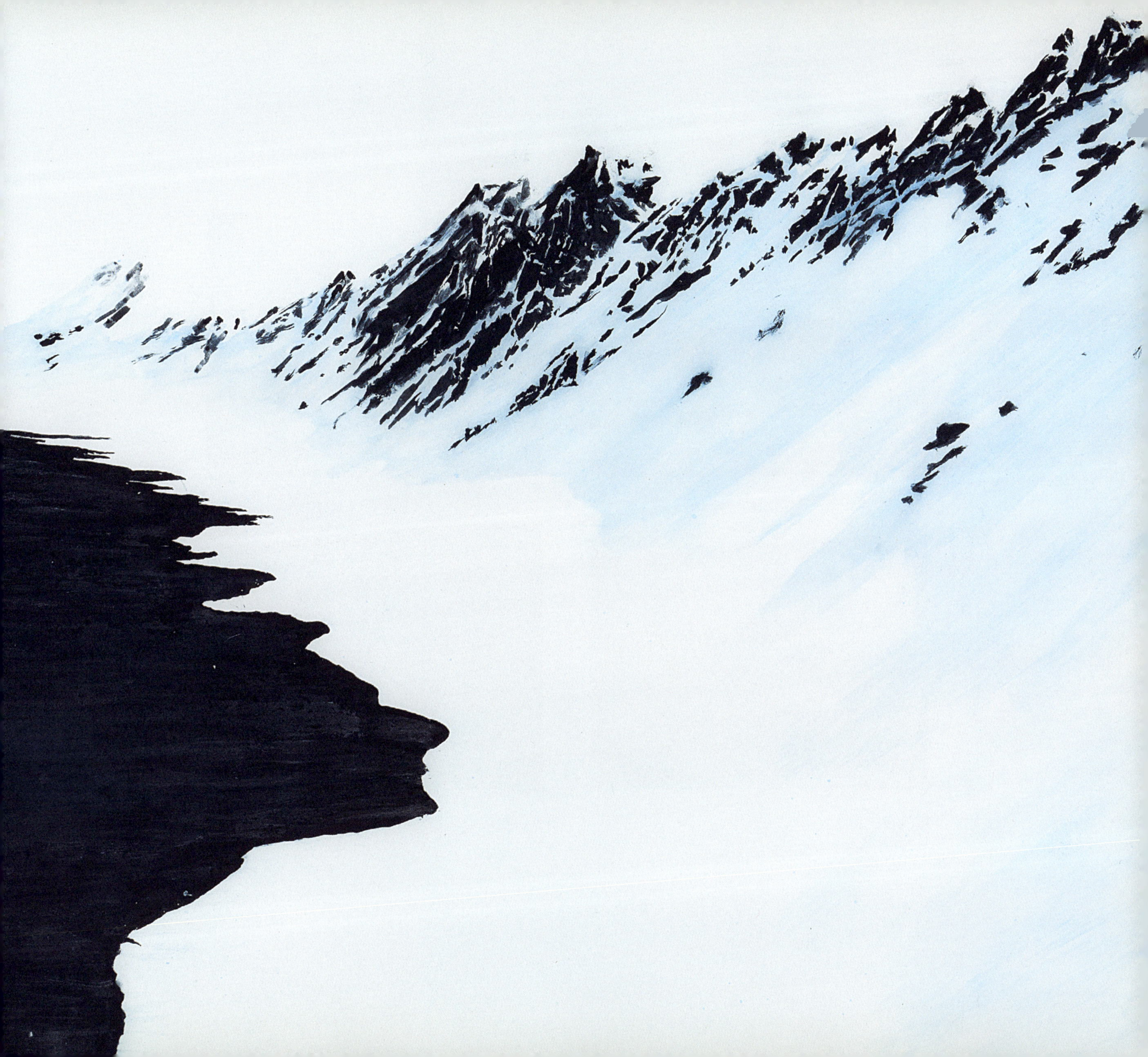

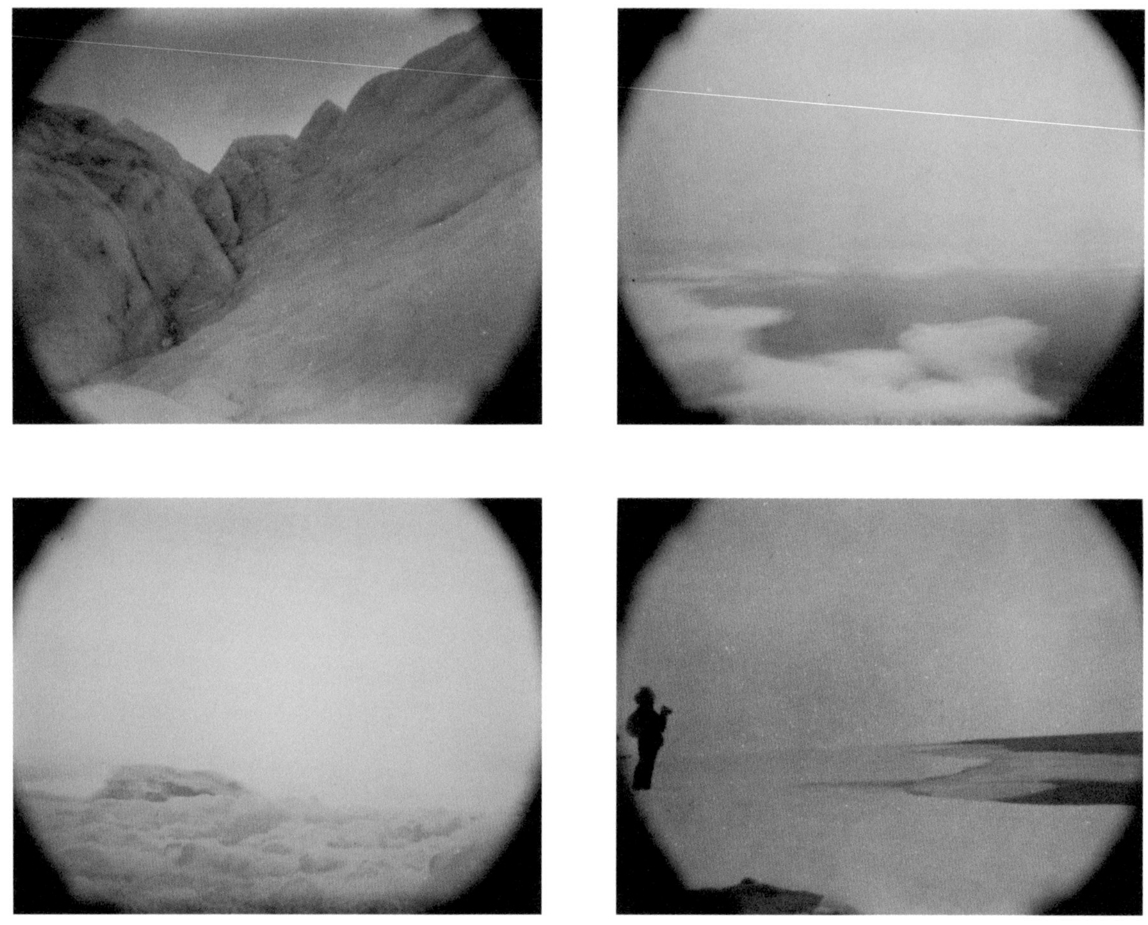

Svalbard and Antarctica, 2024
Pinhole photographic prints on bromide
paper, each 11.3 × 14 cm

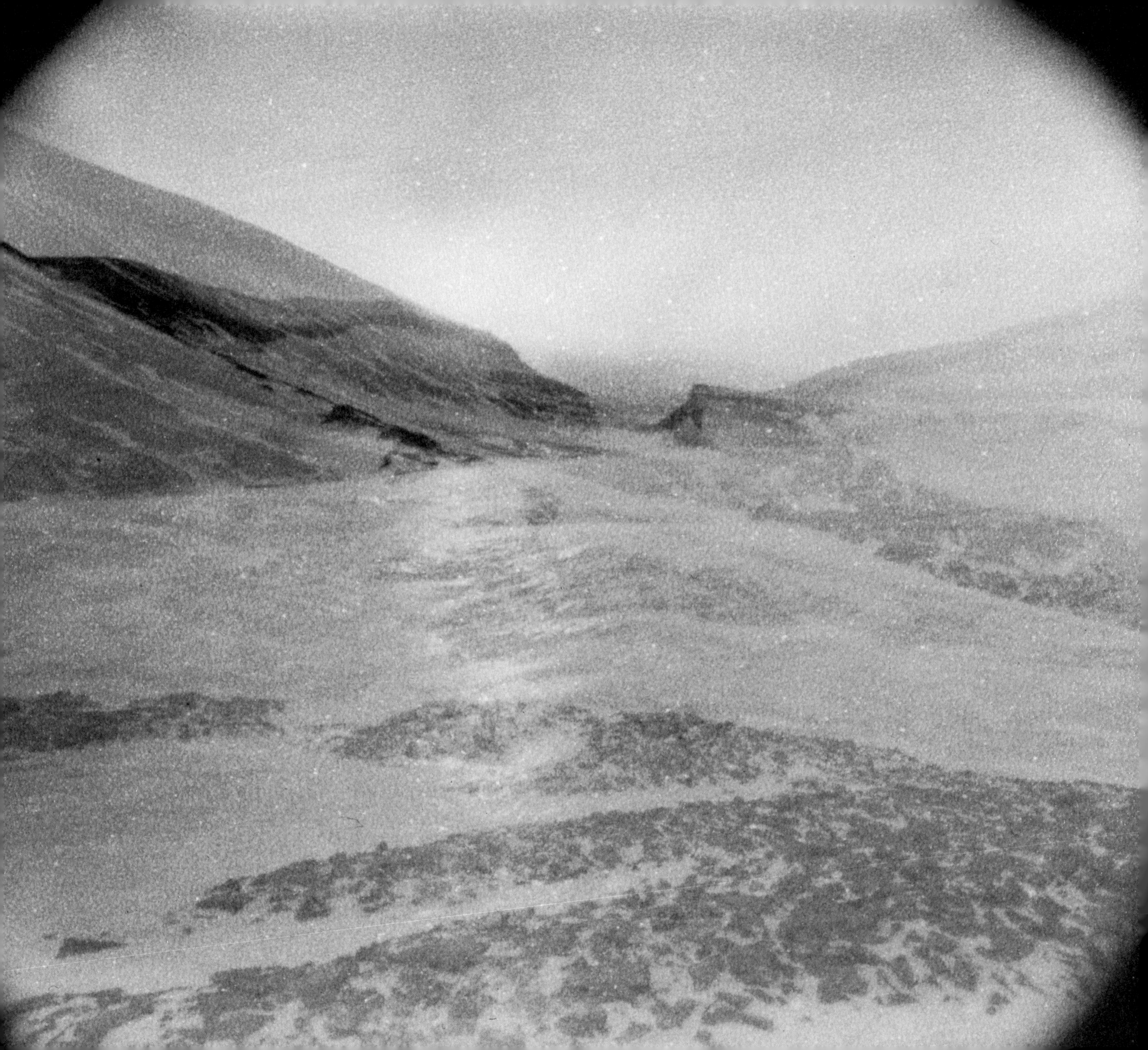

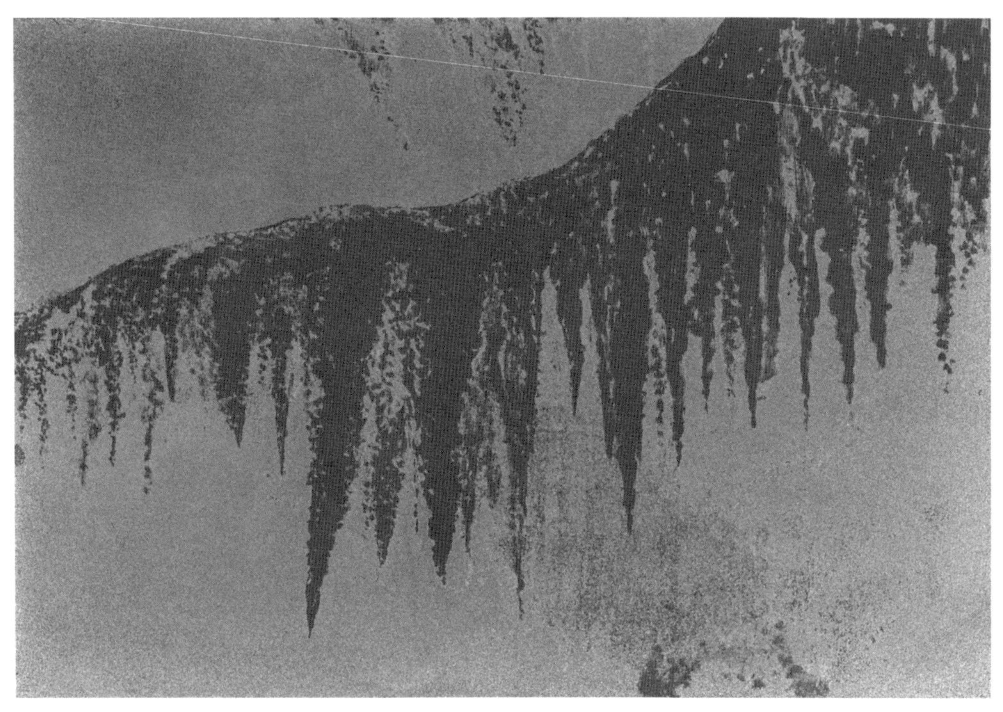

Crevasse Ice I, 2023
Chrome-faced etched copper plate, 30 × 43 cm

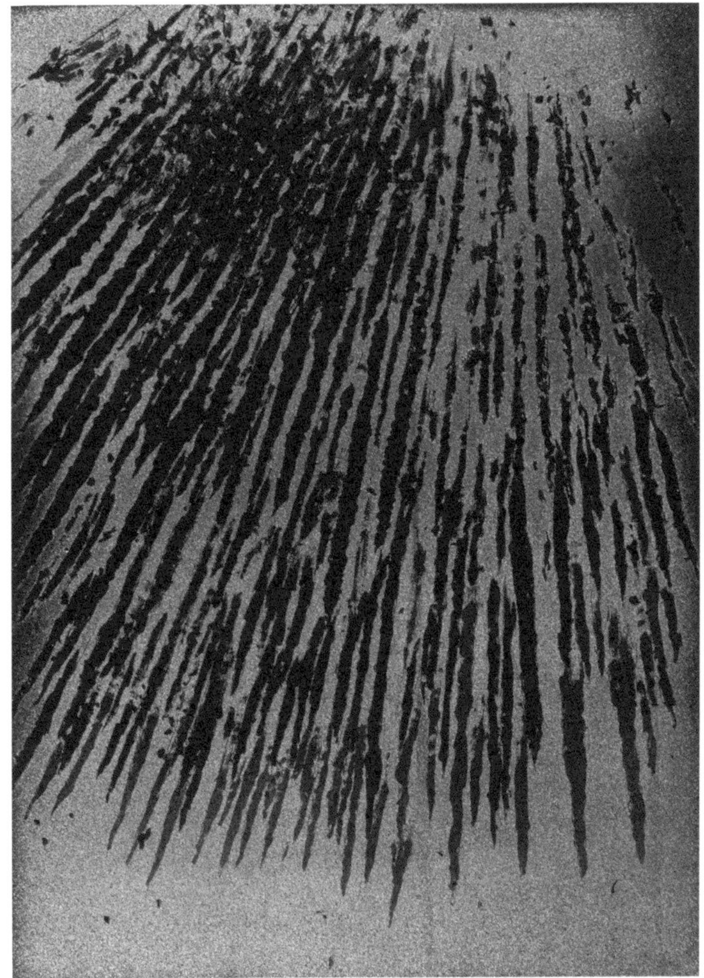

Crevasse Ice II, 2023
Chrome-faced etched copper plate, 43 × 30 cm

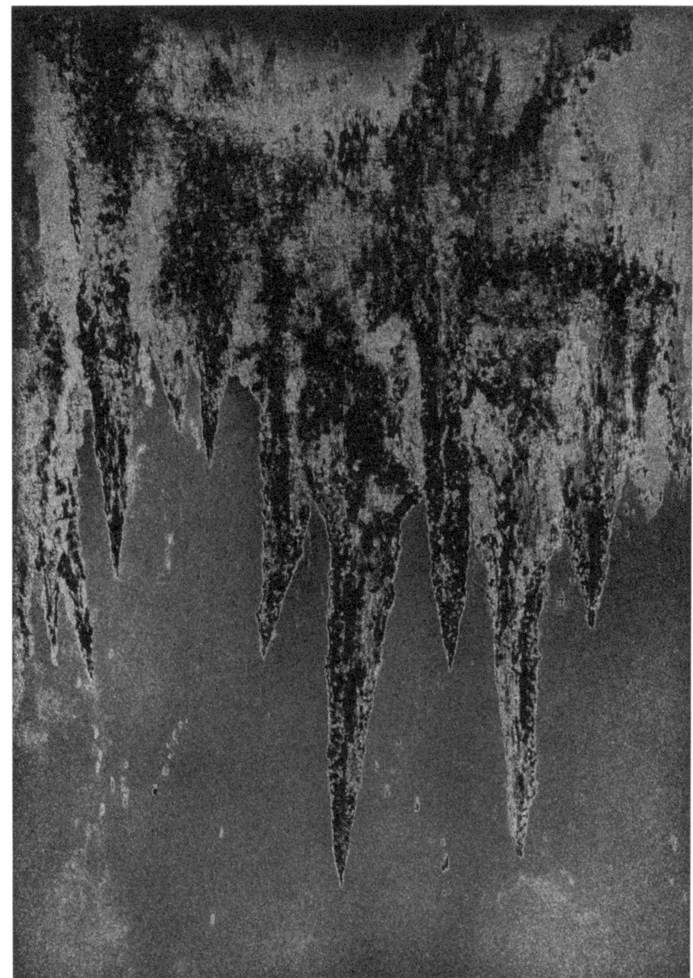

Crevasse Ice III, 2023
Chrome-faced etched copper plate, 43 × 30 cm

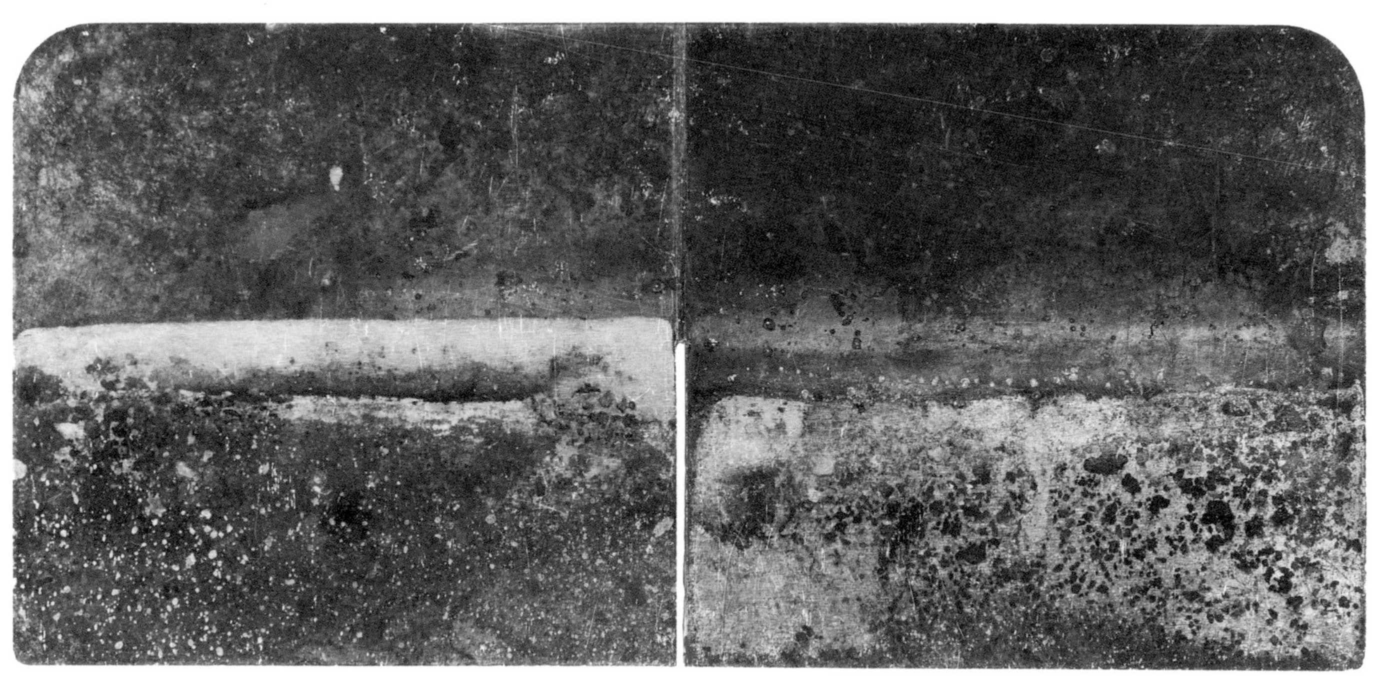

Silver Horizon, 2024
Tarnished aluminium plates, each 8.5 × 17 cm

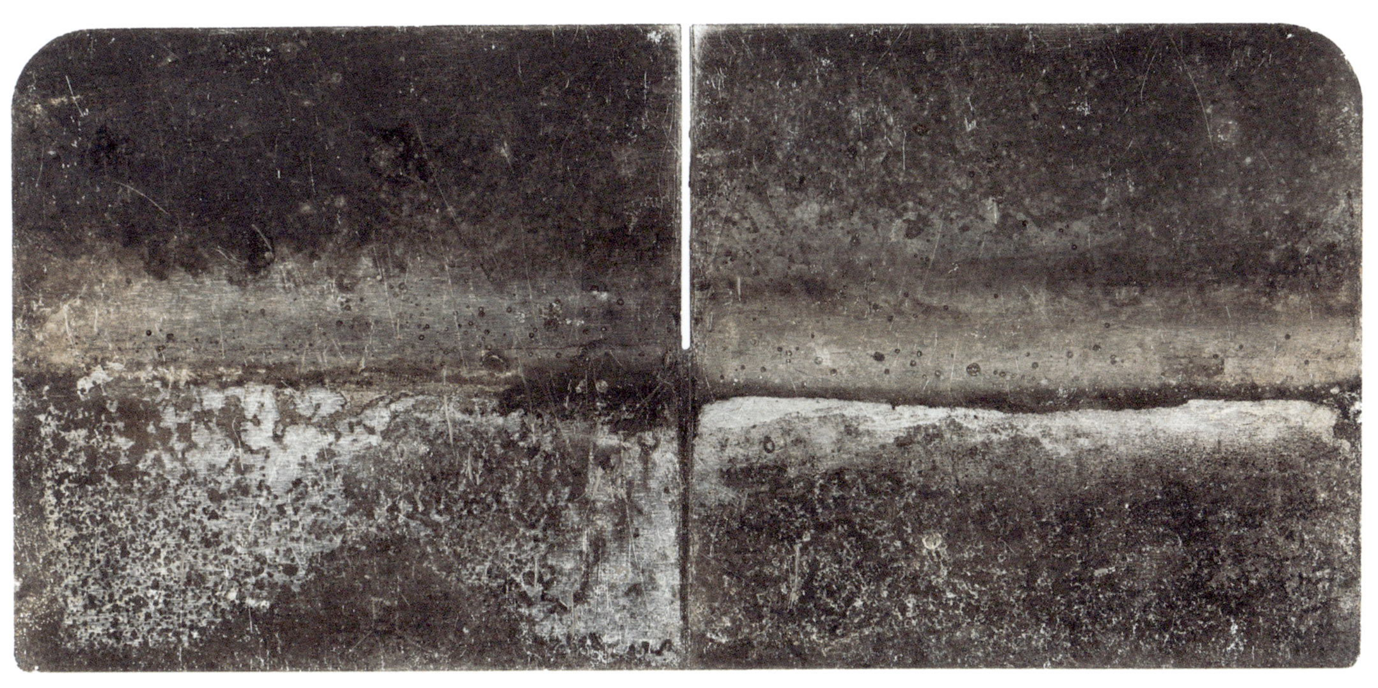

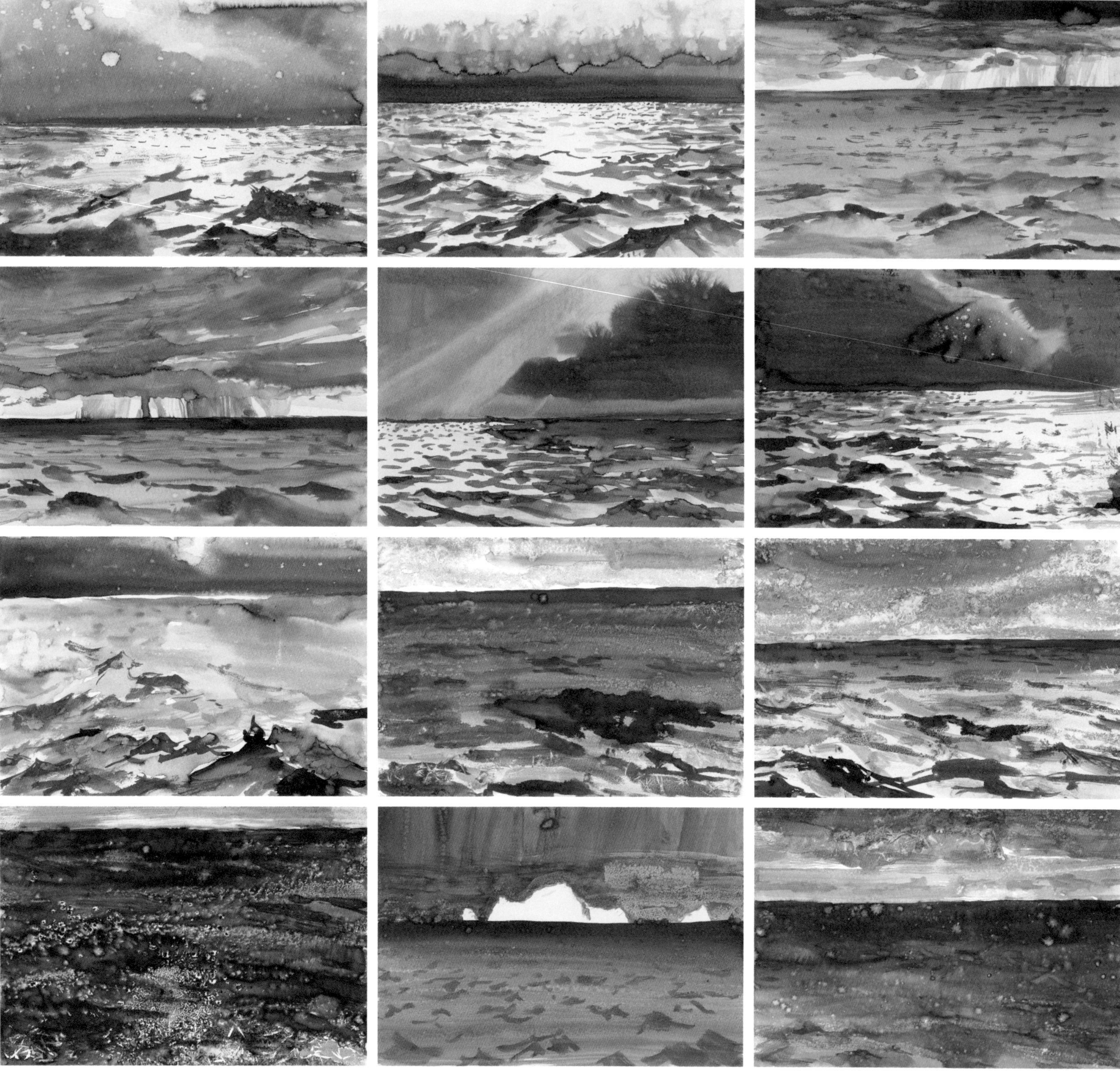

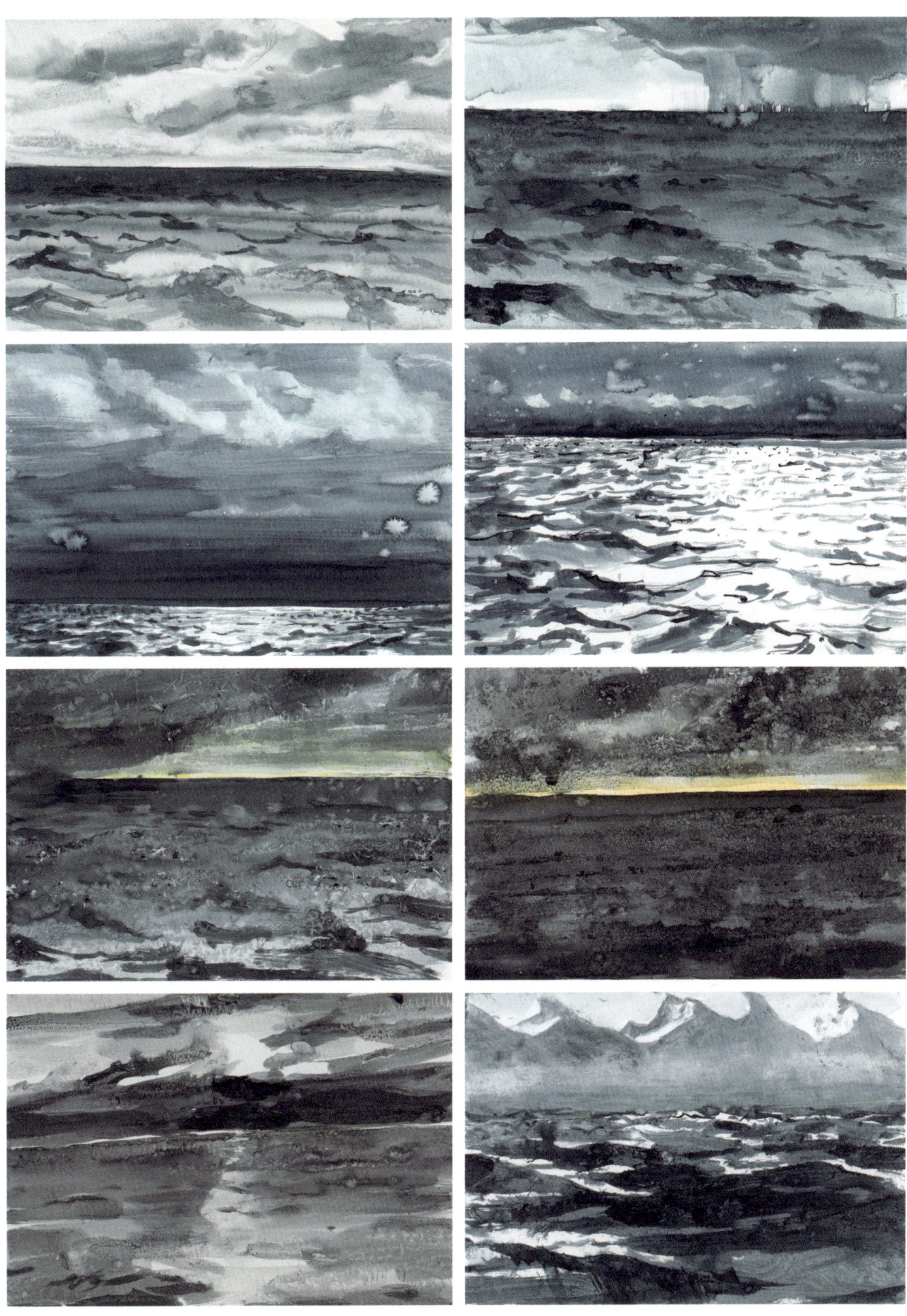

Barents Sea Passage, 2022
Twenty A4 drawings in ink on paper,
88 × 152.5 cm
The drawings were made from left to
right, top to bottom, over a three-day
period. The ship sailed a northerly course
and as it reached sub-zero temperatures
the ink started to freeze on the page.

Overleaf
Breaker, 2023
Ink, sea salt and Eastbourne sea water
on paper, 153 × 342 cm

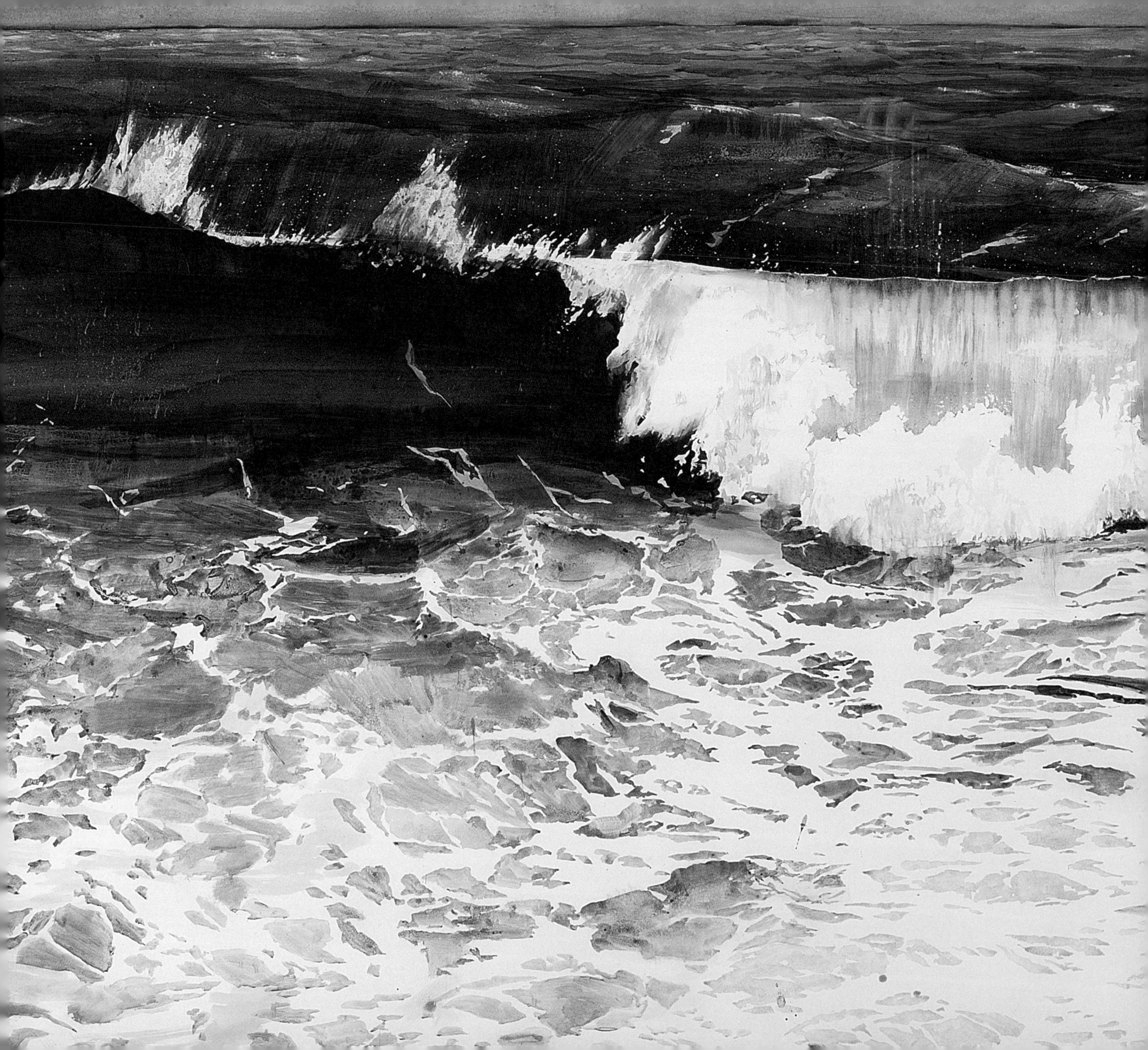

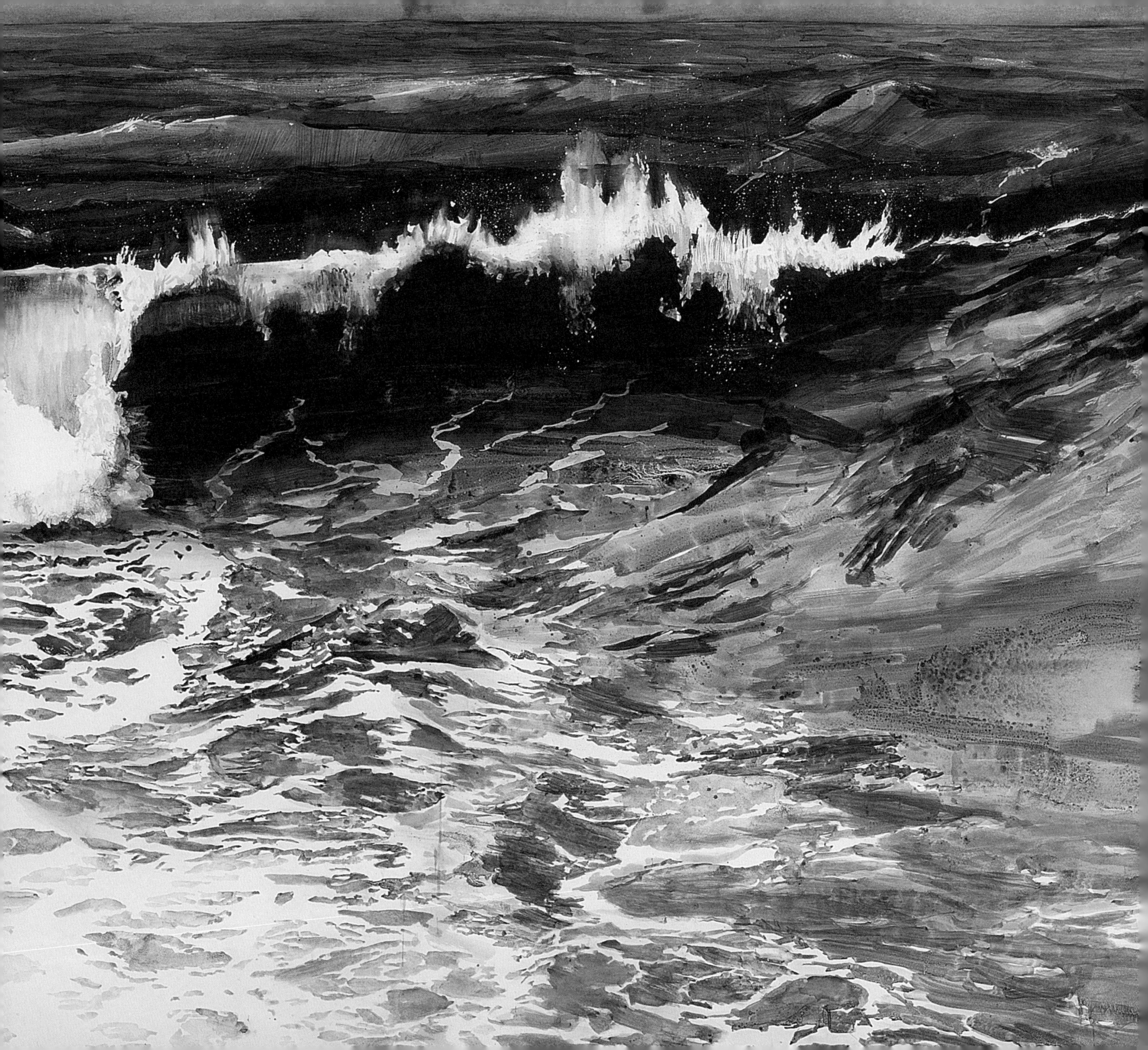

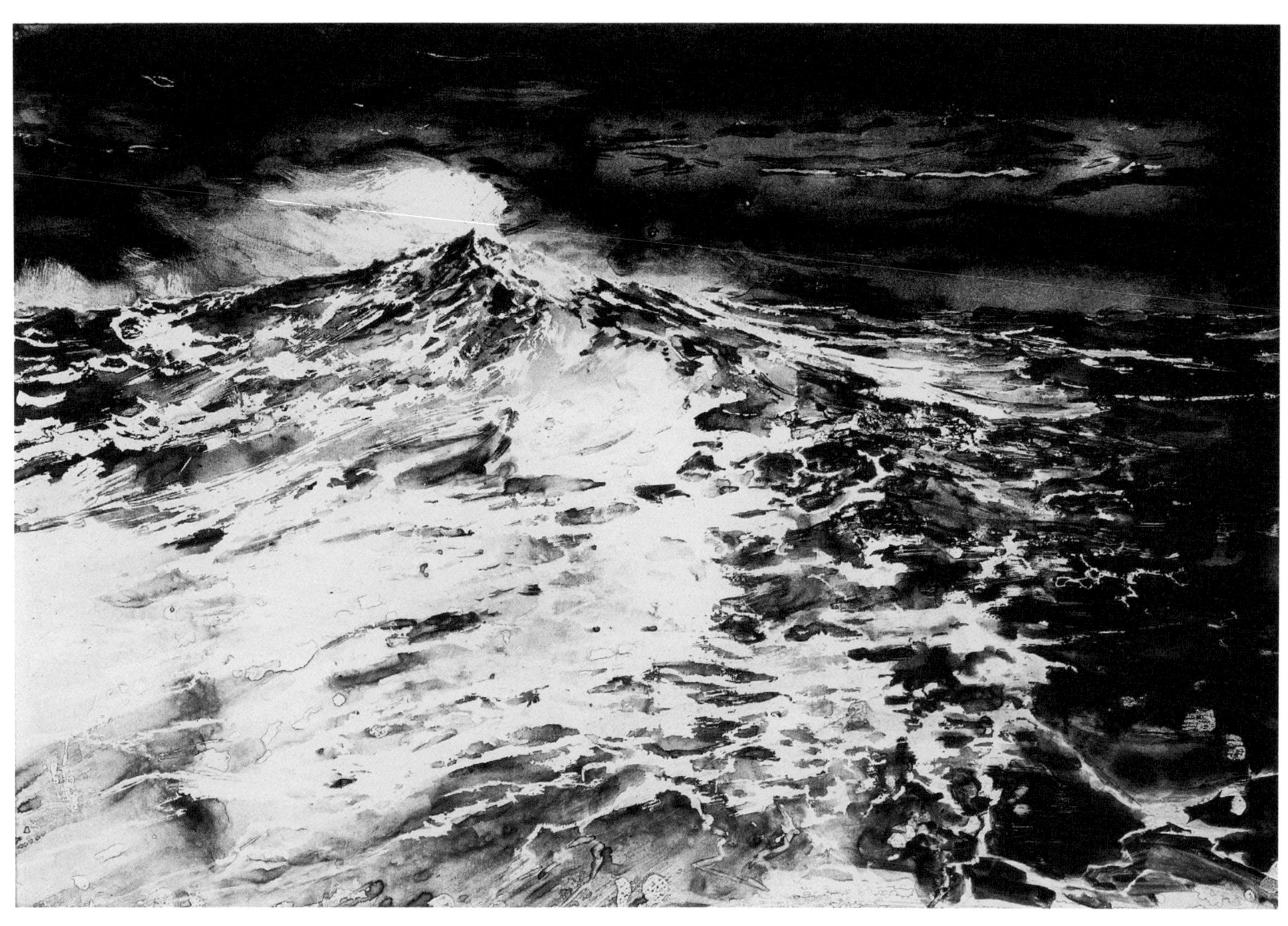

Sea III, 2012
Intaglio print on paper, 45 × 64 cm

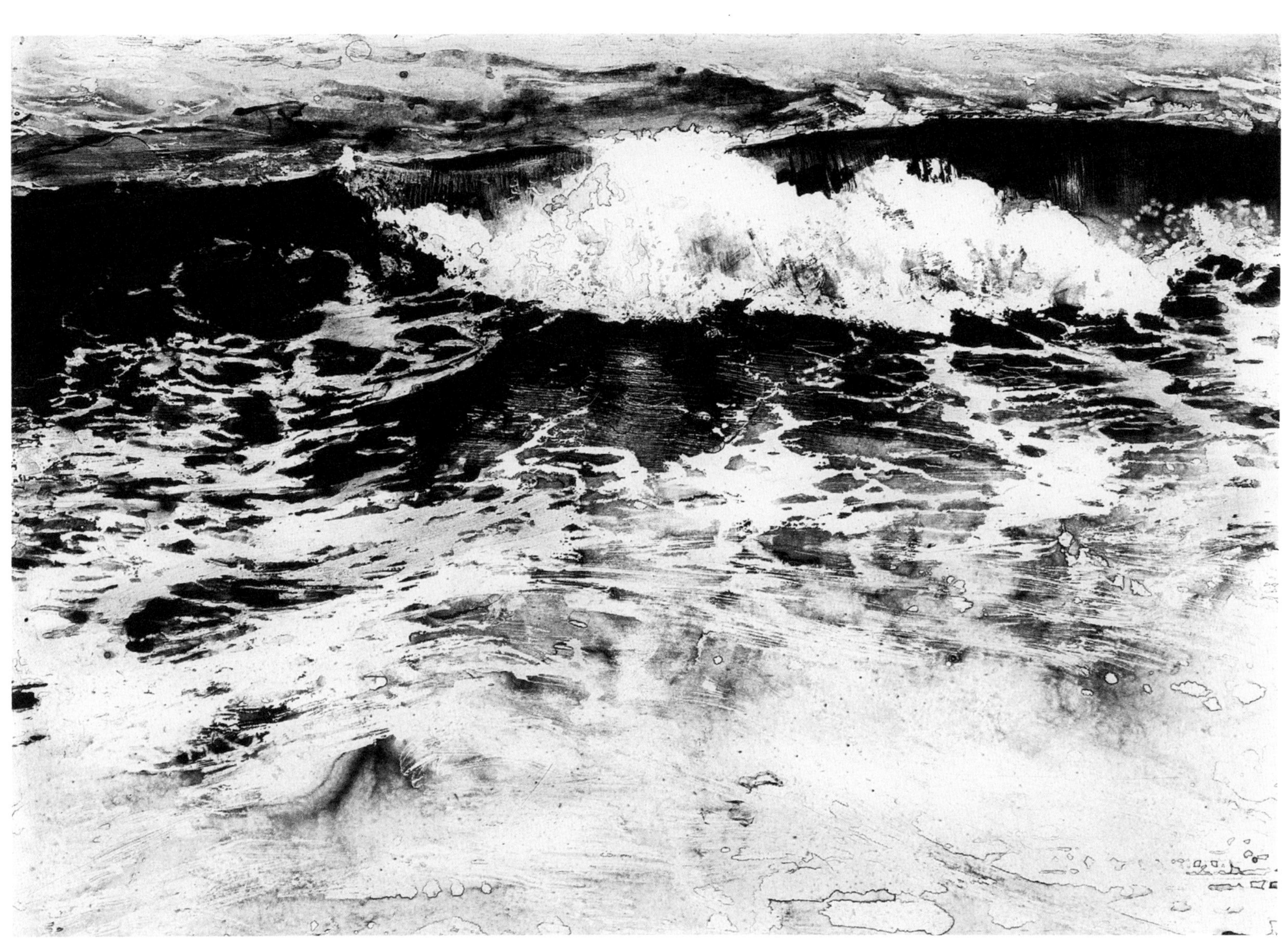

Sea II, 2012
Intaglio print on paper, 48.5 × 68.5 cm

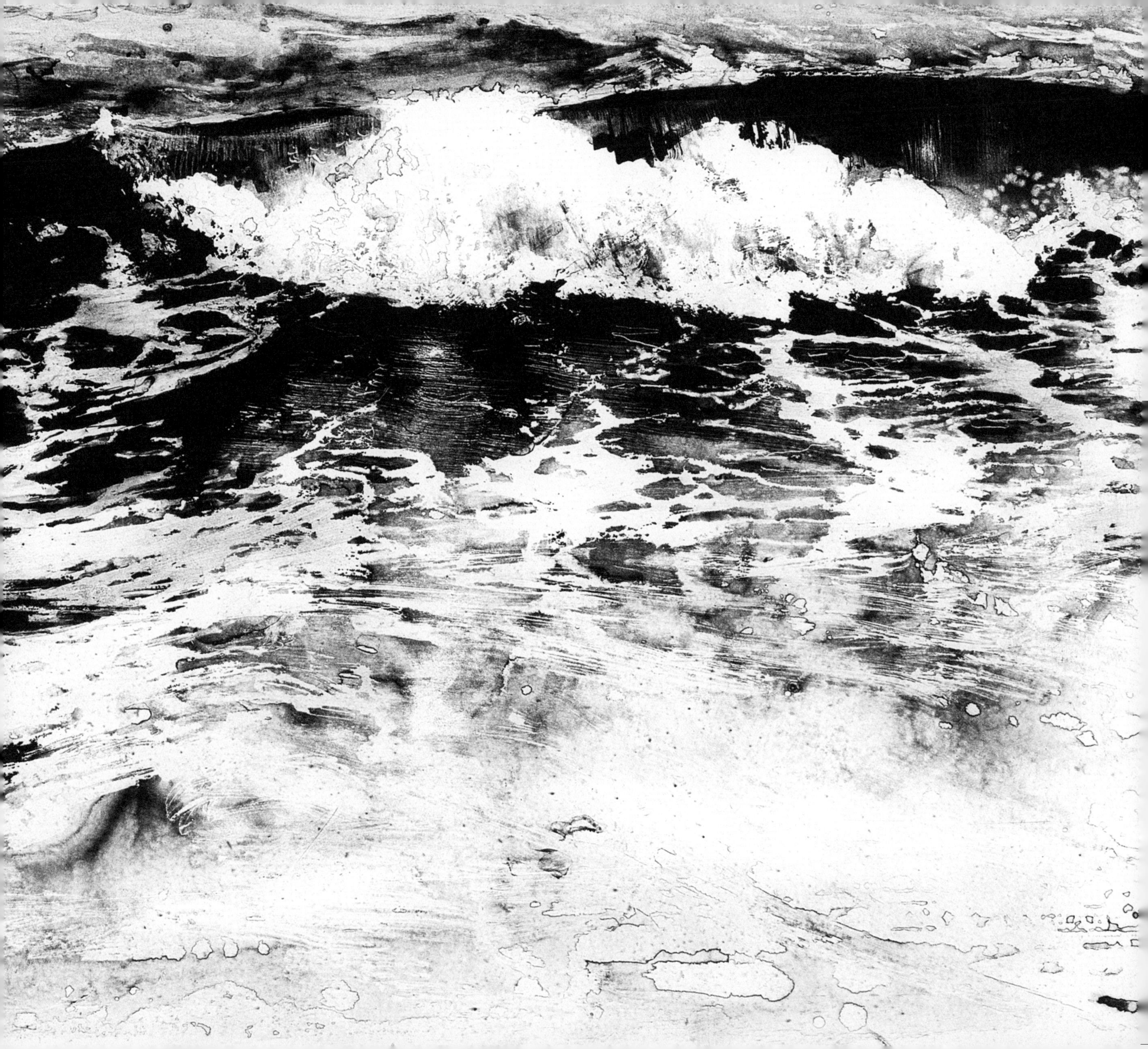

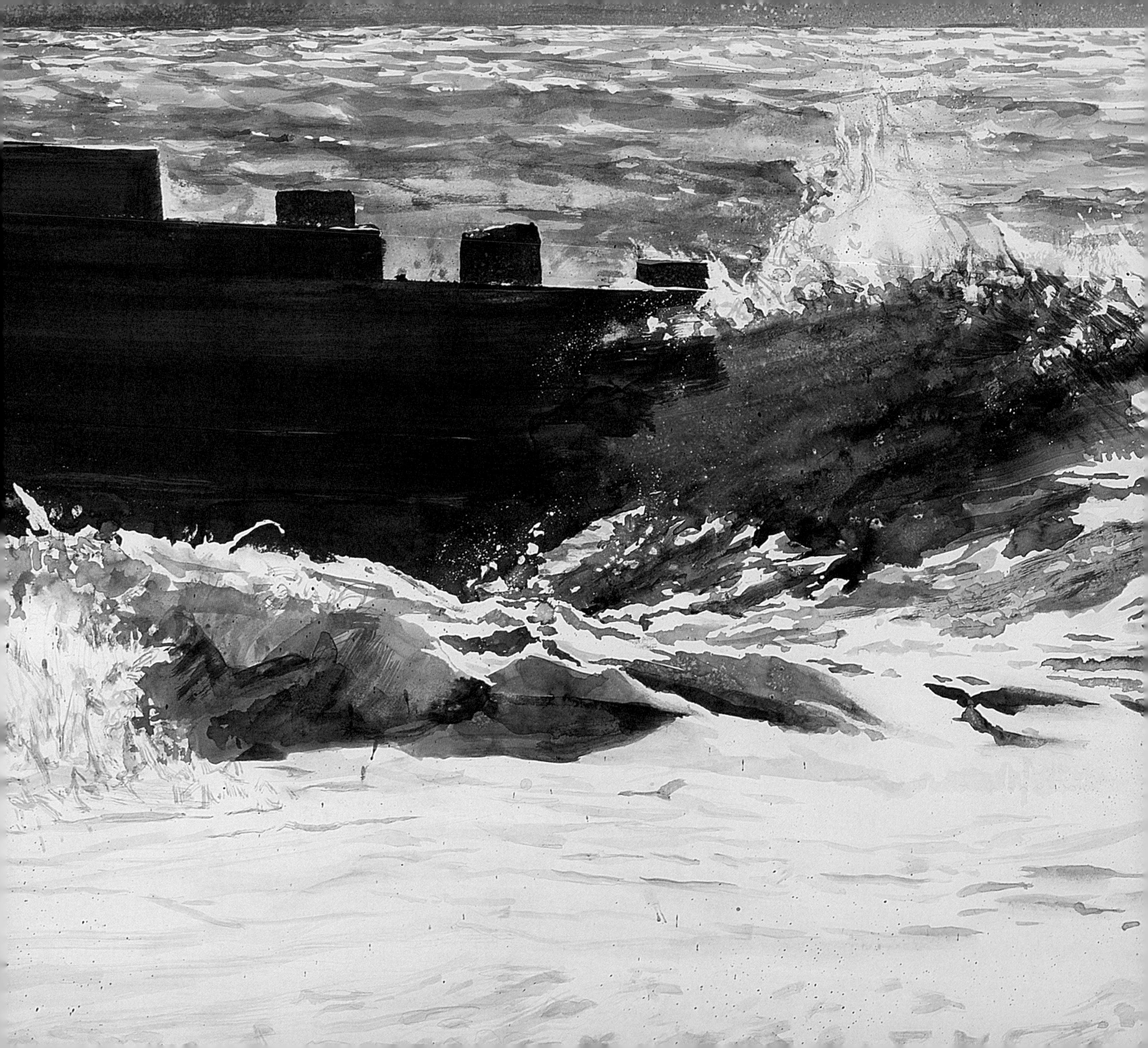

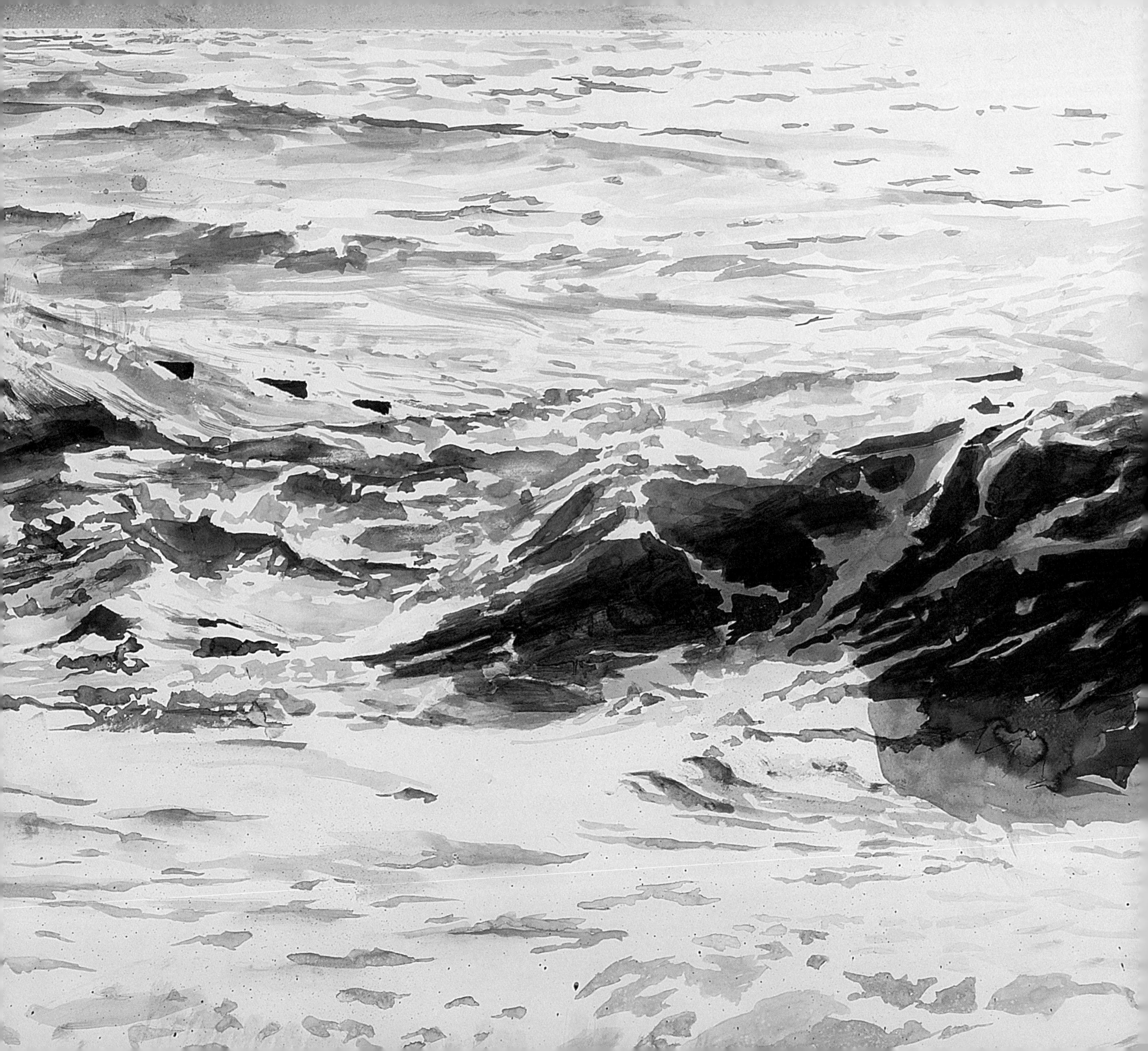

Coastguard Cottages I, Birling Gap, 2023
Ground cliff chalk and fabricated chalk on
black prepared paper, 41 × 57 cm

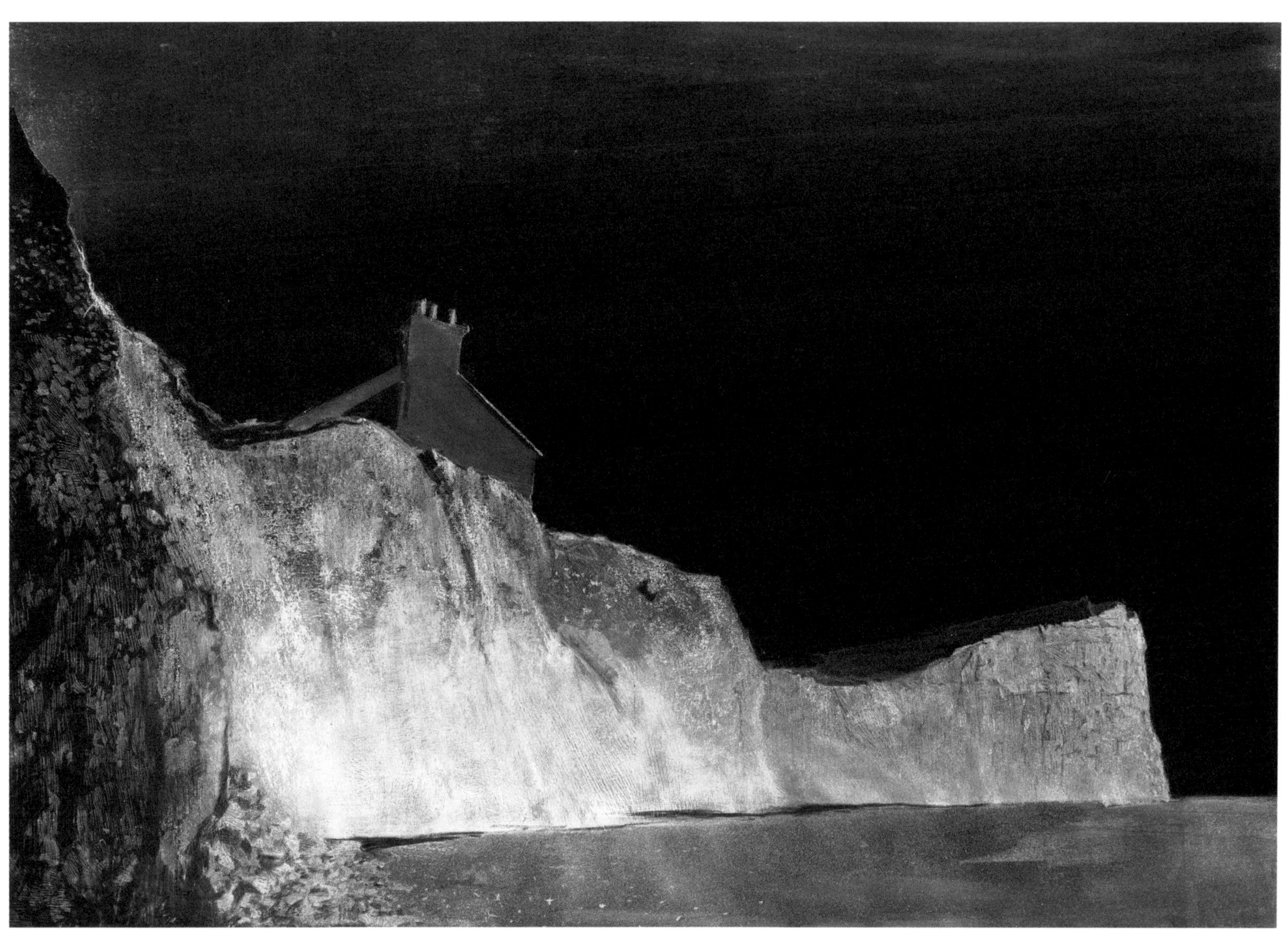

Coastguard Cottages II, Birling Gap, 2023
Ground cliff chalk and fabricated chalk on
black prepared paper, 40.5 × 58.5 cm

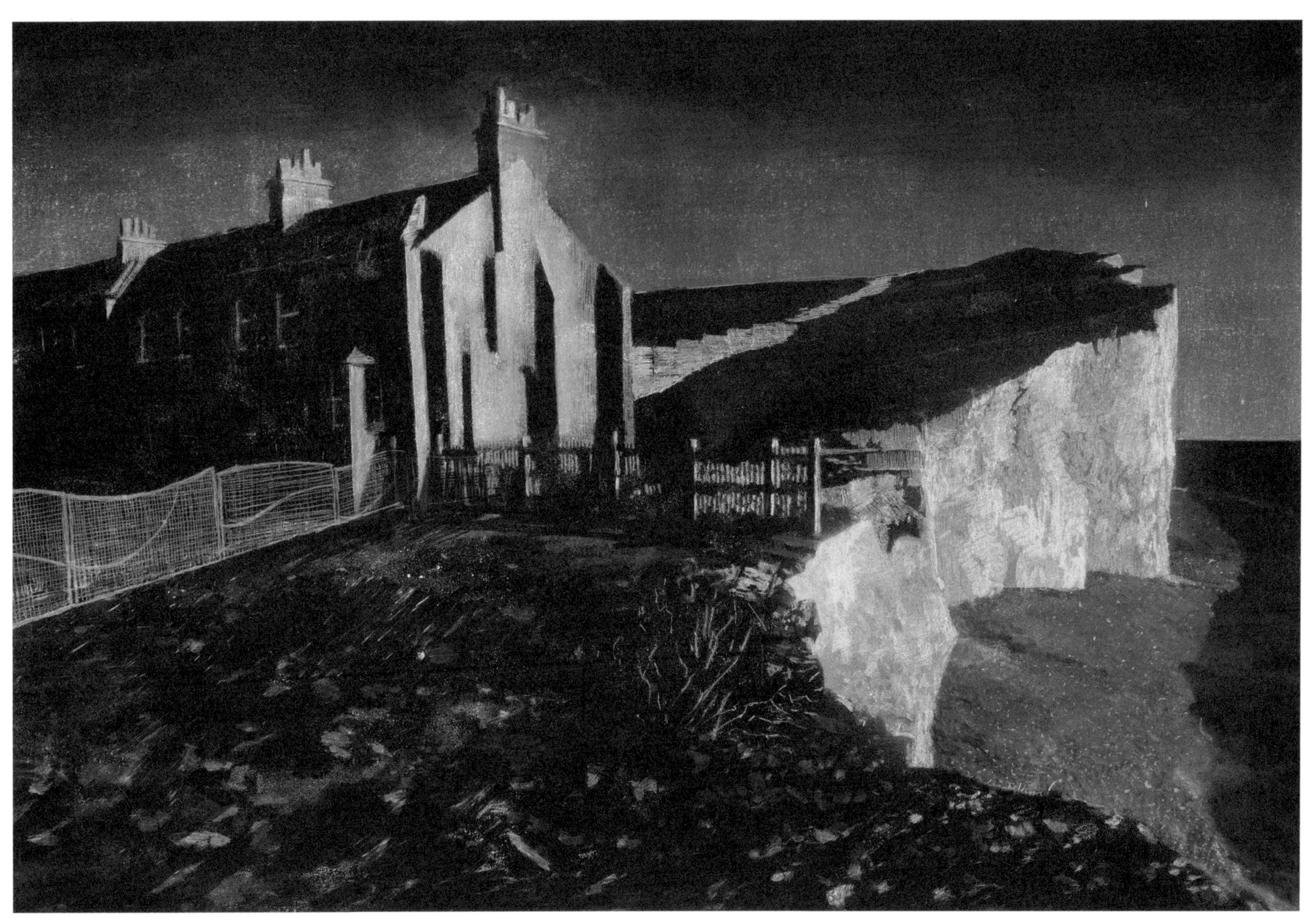

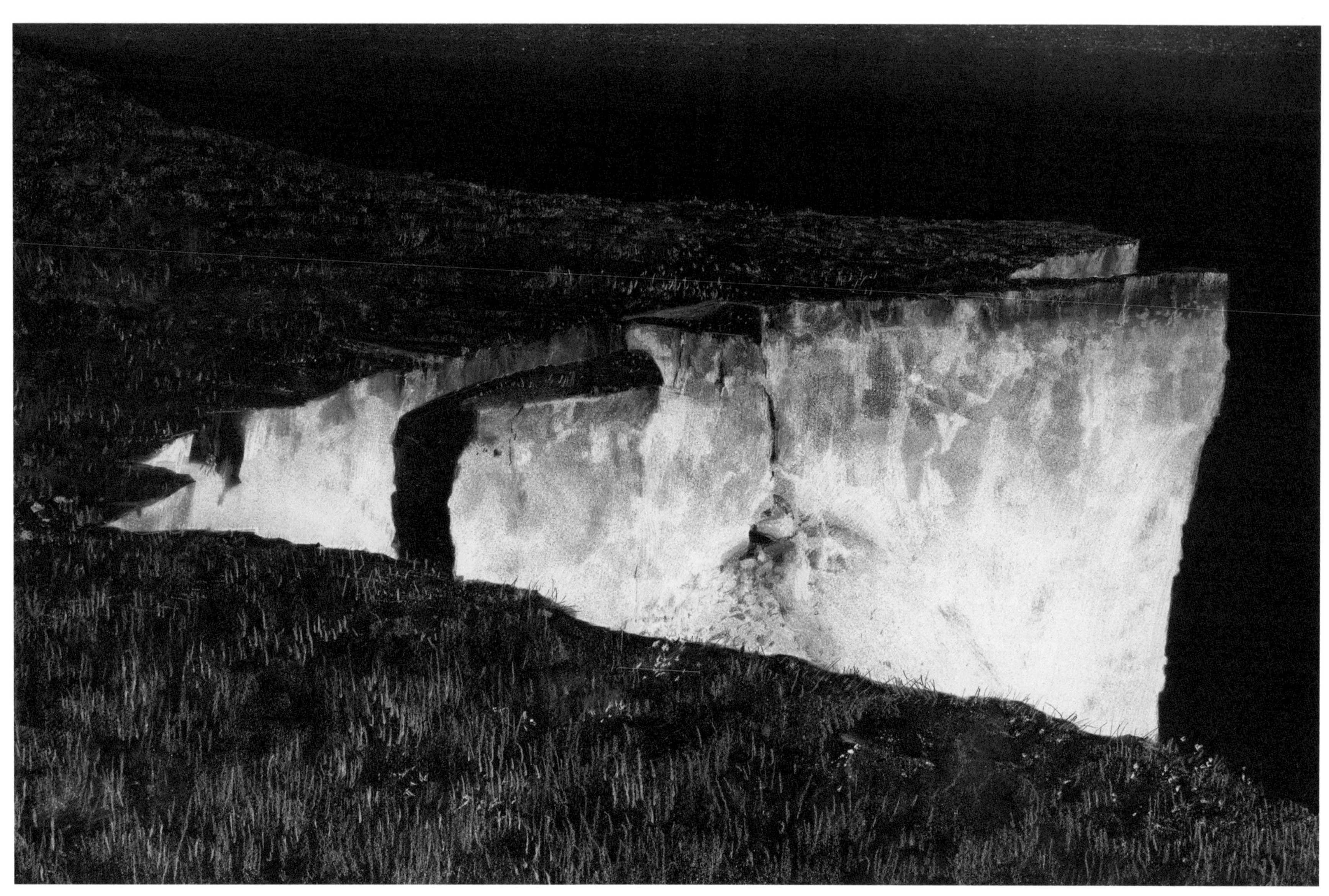

Cliff Crevice, Beachy Head, 2023
Ground cliff chalk and fabricated chalk
on black prepared paper, 42 × 63 cm

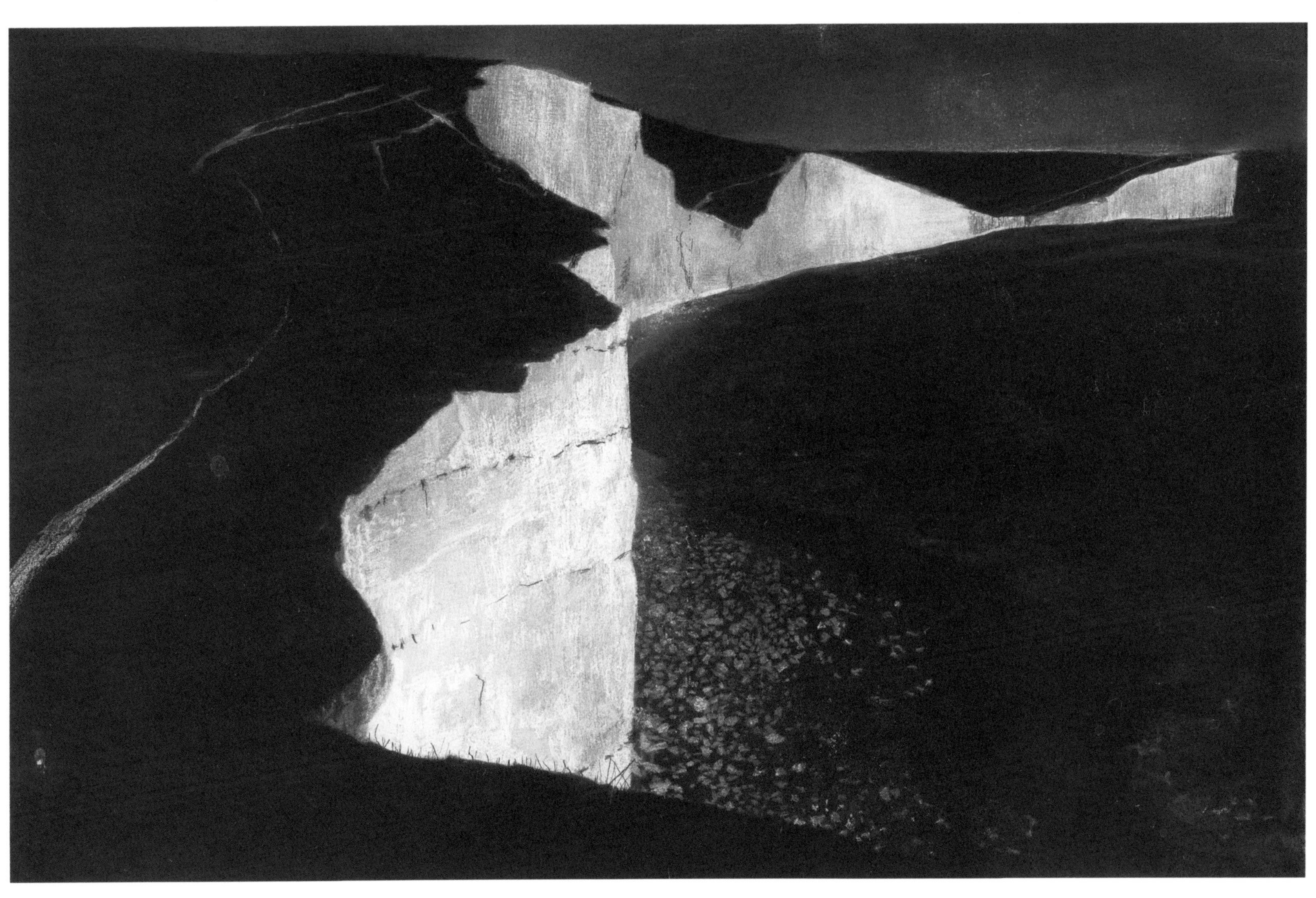

Seven Sisters, 2023
Ground cliff chalk and fabricated chalk
on black prepared paper, 40 × 60.5 cm

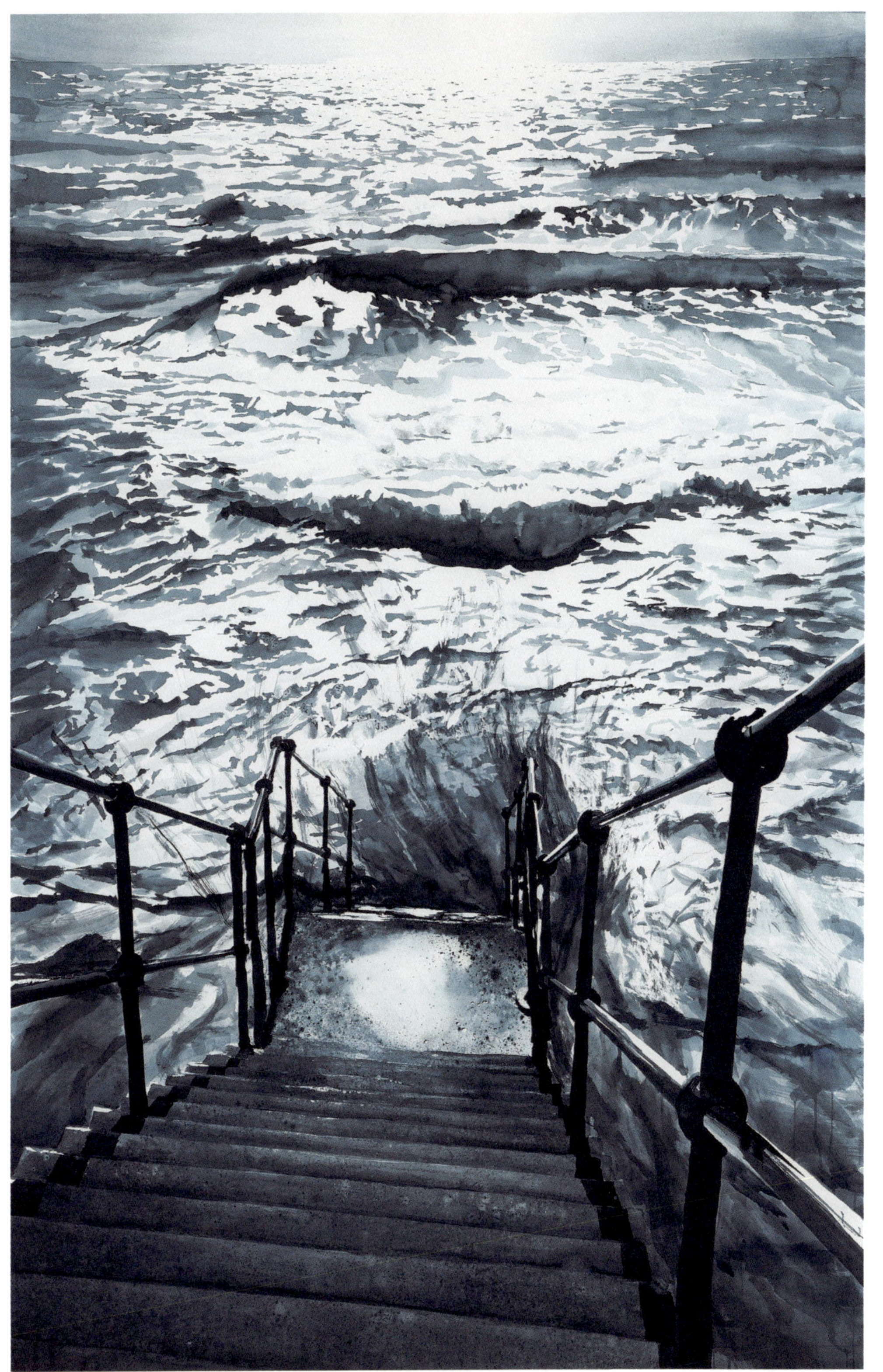

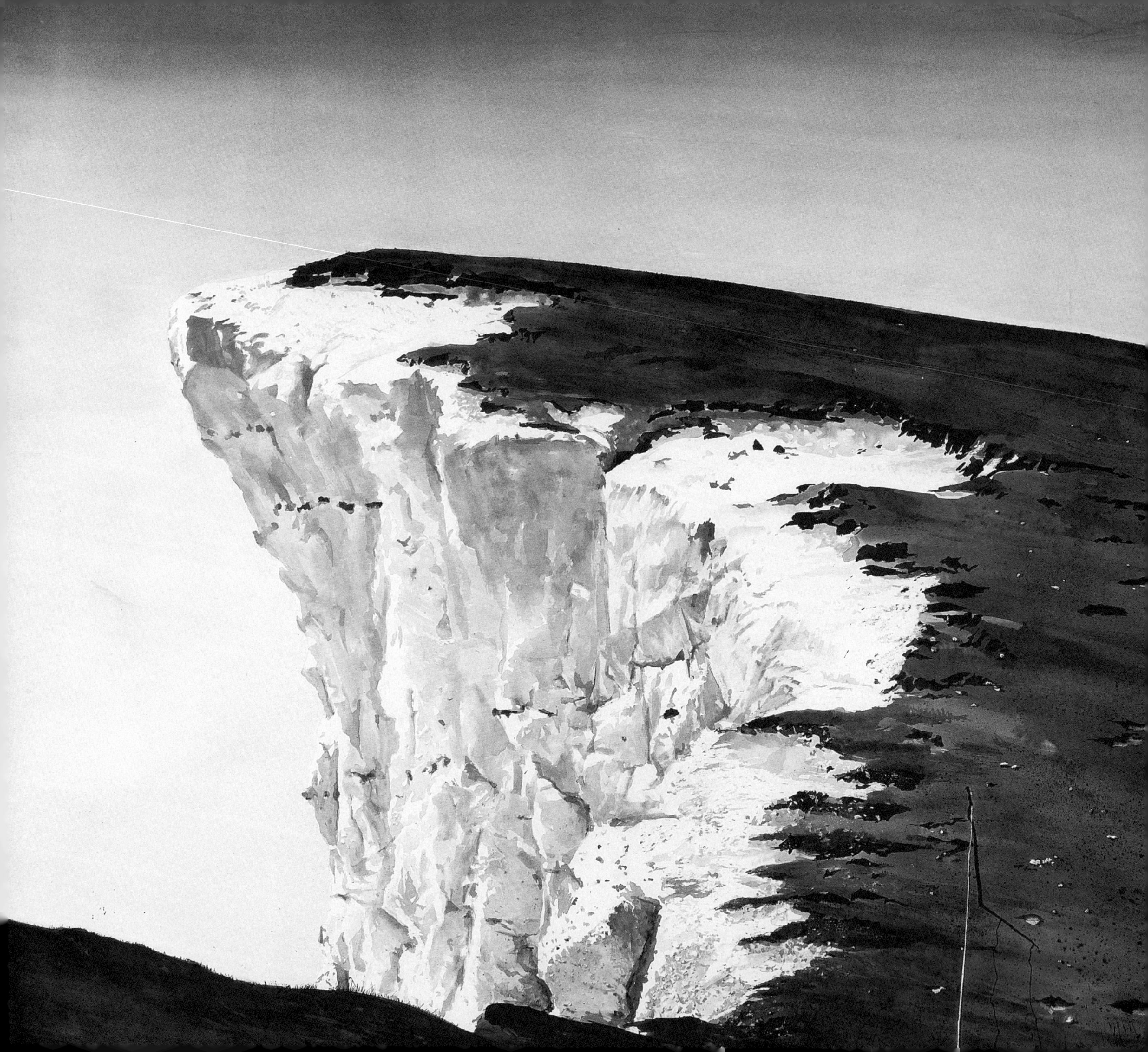

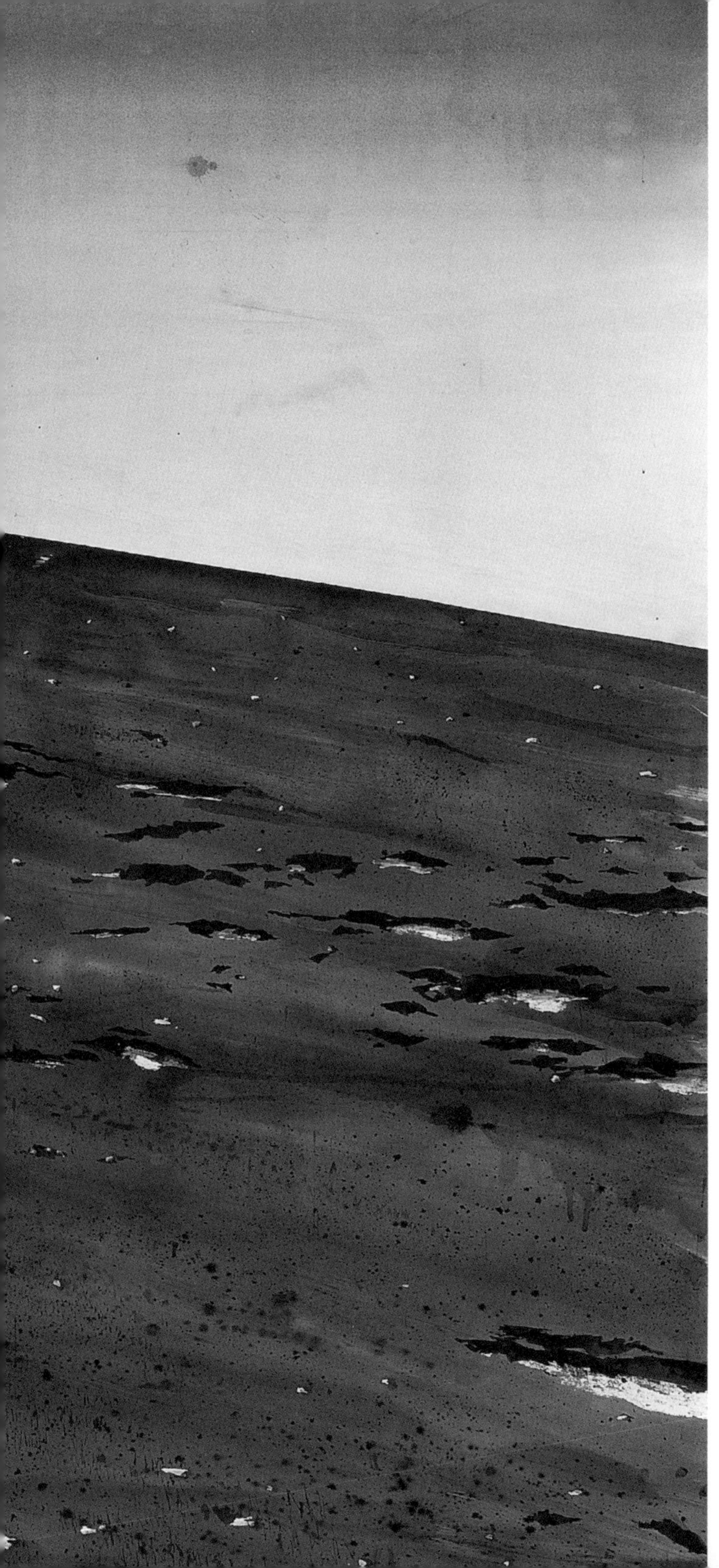

Beachy Head, 2024
Ink on paper, 153 × 236.5 cm

BIOGRAPHY

Emma Stibbon RA's large-scale drawings consider the complexities of extreme environments undergoing transition and change. She often works in such landscapes for extended periods of time, undertaking artist's residencies and participating in expeditions to, among others, Svalbard in the Arctic Circle (2022), Death Valley, California (2019), the Hawaii Volcanoes National Park (2016) and Antarctica (2005, 2013 and 2023). In 2019 she was awarded an Honorary Doctorate of Letters by the University of Bristol for her contribution to the arts. She studied at Goldsmiths, University of London, and the University of the West of England in Bristol. Since 2006 she has been Senior Lecturer at the University of Brighton.

ENDNOTES

Melting Ice | Rising Tides
Emma Stibbon in conversation
with Sara Cooper

1. Walker 2016.
2. Church *et al.* 2007.
3. Arctic Circle artist-in-residence voyage, April 2022: Tromsø to Longyearbyen, Svalbard.
4. Luck and Neter 2023.
5. Brogan 2016.

**The Sublimity
of Boundless Landscapes**
Richard Fisher

1. Burke 2014, p. 67.
2. Kant 2000, p. 129.
3. Dennis 1693, p. 134.
4. Mendelssohn 1997, p. 195.
5. Addison 1712.
6. Stibbon 2021.
7. Burke 2014, p. 59.
8. Seaford Town Council 2023.

BIBLIOGRAPHIC SOURCES AND FURTHER READING

Addison 1712
Joseph Addison, 'The Pleasures of the Imagination', *The Spectator*, no. 412, 23 June 1712

Berlin 2005
Ian Monroe and Emma Stibbon: Utopian Architecture, exh. cat., upstairs berlin, 2005

Berlin 2007
Stéphane Biesenbach, *Emma Stibbon: Antarctica*, exh. cat., upstairs berlin, 2007

Berlin 2009
Andreas Tetlow and Carolyn Wilde (eds), *Emma Stibbon: StadtLandschaften*, exh. cat., Stadtmuseum Berlin, 2009

Bristol 2022
Christina Payne, Nathalie Levi and Emma Stibbon, *Earth: Digging Deep in British Art 1781–2022*, exh. cat., Royal West of England Academy, Bristol, 2022

Brogan 2016
Caroline Brogan, 'Cliff Erosion Rates in Sussex Have Accelerated Ten-fold in the Past 200 Years', Imperial College London, 15 November 2016: www.tinyurl.com/6rk4t3kp

Burke 2014
Edmund Burke, *A Philosophical Enquiry into the Origin of Our Ideas of the Sublime and Beautiful* [1757], Cambridge, 2014

Campbell 2015
Nancy Campbell, 'Postcards from the Edge of the Earth: Emma Stibbon's Polar Art', Royal Academy of Arts, London, 18 June 2015: www.tinyurl.com/2xyezayc

Casey and Davis 2020
Sarah Casey and Gerry Davis (eds), *Drawing Investigations: Graphic Relationships with Science, Culture, and Environment*, London, 2020

Church *et al.* 2007
John A. Church, John E. Hay and Vivien Gornitz, 'Ice and Sea Level Change', in United Nations Environmental Programme, *Global Outlook for Ice and Snow*, 2007: www.tinyurl.com/2asmuka5

Dennis 1693
John Dennis, 'A Journey Over the Alpes', *Miscellanies in Verse and Prose*, London, 1693

Kant 2000
Immanuel Kant, *Critique of the Power of Judgement* [1790], trans. Paul Guyer and Eric Matthews, Cambridge, 2000

London 2017
Helen Waters and Emma Stibbon (eds), *Emma Stibbon: Volcano*, exh. cat., Cristea Roberts Gallery, London, 2017

Luck and Neter 2023
Flaminia Luck and Hanna Neter, 'Cliff Erosion Forces Building's Partial Demolition', BBC News, 23 November 2023: www.tinyurl.com/bdhm82jj

Marlborough 2013
Terra Infirma: A Landscape in Flux, Drawings of Iceland, exh. cat., Rabley Drawing Centre, Marlborough, 2013

Marlborough 2019
Gill Saunders *et al.* (eds), *Emma Stibbon: Territories of Print, 1994–2019*, exh. cat., Rabley Drawing Centre, Marlborough, 2019

Mendelssohn 1997
Moses Mendelssohn, 'On the Sublime and the Naïve in the Fine Sciences' [1758], in *Moses Mendelssohn: Philosophical Writings*, trans. Daniel O. Dahlstrom, Cambridge, 1997

San Diego 2023
Desert Sublime: Southwestern Landscapes, exh. cat., Humanities Center Gallery, University of San Diego, 2023: www.tinyurl.com/5ybpazdz

Seaford Town Council 2023
Seaford Town Council, 'Hope Gap Steps Update', 14 November 2023: www.seafordtowncouncil.gov.uk/council/hope-gap-steps-update

Stibbon 2006
Emma Stibbon, 'In Search of the Sublime', *Printmaking Today*, no. 15, Winter 2006, pp. 8–9

Stibbon 2019
Emma Stibbon, *Fire and Ice*, Royal Academy of Arts, London, 2019

Stibbon 2021
Emma Stibbon, *In Search of the Sublime*, BBC Radio 3, 5 December 2021: www.bbc.co.uk/programmes/m00126vd

Stibbon and Cashman 2021
Emma Stibbon and Katharine Cashman (eds), *An Art and Science Collaboration, 2013–2021*, Bristol, 2021

Walker 2016
Peter Walker, 'Iconic White Cliffs of Southern England Eroding "10 Times Faster" than Over Last Few Thousand Years', *Independent*, 8 November 2016

York 2019
Suzanne Fagence-Cooper and Richard Johns (eds), *Ruskin, Turner and the Storm Cloud*, exh. cat., York Art Gallery and Abbot Hall Art Gallery, Kendal, 2019

SELECTED SOLO EXHIBITIONS

2023
'Desert Sublime: Southwestern Landscapes', Humanities Center Gallery, University of San Diego

2022
'Vanishing Point', Galerie Bastian, Berlin

2019
'Fire and Ice', Cristea Roberts Gallery, London
'Ruskin, Turner and the Storm Cloud', York Art Gallery and Abbot Hall Art Gallery, Kendal
'Territories of Print 1994–2019', Rabley Drawing Centre, Marlborough

2017
'Emma Stibbon: Volcano', Cristea Roberts Gallery, London

2016
'Uncertain Ground', Galerie Bastian, Berlin

2015
'Ice Limit', Polar Museum, Cambridge
'Ice Mirage', Galerie Bastian, Berlin

2013
'Terra Infirma: A Landscape in Flux, Drawings of Iceland', Rabley Drawing Centre, Marlborough

2009
'Emma Stibbon: StadtLandschaften', Stadtmuseum Berlin

2008
'Glacial Shift', Polar Museum, University of Cambridge

2007
'Emma Stibbon: Antarctica', upstairs berlin

PUBLIC COLLECTIONS

Berlin
Potsdam Museum
Stadtmuseum Berlin

Bournemouth
Russell-Cotes Art Gallery and Museum

Bristol
Bristol Museum and Art Gallery

Cambridge
Fitzwilliam Museum
Polar Museum, University of Cambridge

Chichester
Pallant House Gallery

Eastbourne
Towner Eastbourne

London
British Academy
Royal Academy of Arts
Victoria and Albert Museum

Newcastle upon Tyne
Laing Art Gallery

New Haven
Yale University Art Gallery

San Diego
University of San Diego

UK
Government Art Collection

Walsall
New Art Gallery Walsall

INDEX OF WORKS ILLUSTRATED

First published on the occasion of the exhibition

'Emma Stibbon, Melting Ice | Rising Tides'
9 May – 15 September 2024

Exhibition curated by Sara Cooper

Towner Eastbourne
Sara Cooper, Head of Collections and Exhibitions

Joe Hill, Director and CEO

Karen Taylor, Collections and Exhibitions Curator

Royal Academy Publications
Florence Dassonville, Production and Distribution Co-ordinator

Carola Krueger, Production and Distribution Manager

Peter Sawbridge, Head of Publishing and Editorial Director

Copy-editing and proofreading: Caroline Ellerby

Design: JMG Studio

Colour origination and print: Gomer Press, Wales, on FSC-certified materials, with print and paper carbon-balanced through the World Land Trust

Editorial note
All works of art are by Emma Stibbon RA unless otherwise stated.

Dimensions of all works of art are given in centimetres, height before width.

Frontispiece and opposite: *Barents Sea Passage*, 2022 (details), see pages 52–53

Page 2: *Ice Front I*, 2020 (detail), see page 31

Page 4: *Hope Gap*, 2022 (detail), see page 69

Pages 14–15: *Sea Ice, Svalbard*, 2023 (detail), see pages 28–29

Acknowledgements
Emma Stibbon RA and Towner Eastbourne would like to thank the following for their invaluable assistance: Meryl Ainslie; Aeneas Bastian; Bastian Gallery; Amy-Jane Blackhall; University of Brighton; Bristol Old Vic; Kathy Cashman; Cristea Roberts Gallery; The Devonshire Collections, Chatsworth; Tristan Duke; Richard Fisher; Ink on Paper Press; Marcus Jefferies; Andrew Johnson; Caroline Lucas MP; Mariele Neudecker; Tim Pearse; Spike Island; Spike Print Studio; Nancy Stephens; Cliff Thorn; Helen Waters.

Photographic acknowledgements
Unless otherwise stated, all works of art are copyright Emma Stibbon RA.

Stuart Bunce Photography: pages 2, 4, 8 (right), 11, 14–71. Photo: Tristan Duke: page 12. Photo: Rob Harris: poster of *Cliff Fall*. Racquet Studios: page 9 (bottom). Copyright J. Salmon Image Archive: page 9 (top). Photo: Towner Eastbourne: page 8 (left).

Every attempt has been made to trace photographic acknowledgements. We apologise for any inadvertent infringement and invite appropriate rights holders to contact us.

British Library Cataloguing-in-Publication Data
A catalogue record for this book is available from the British Library

ISBN 978-1-915815-05-7

Distributed outside the United States and Canada by ACC Art Books Ltd, Riverside House, Dock Lane, Melton, Woodbridge, IP12 IPE

Distributed in the United States and Canada by ARTBOOK | D.A.P., 75 Broad Street, Suite 630, New York, NY 10004

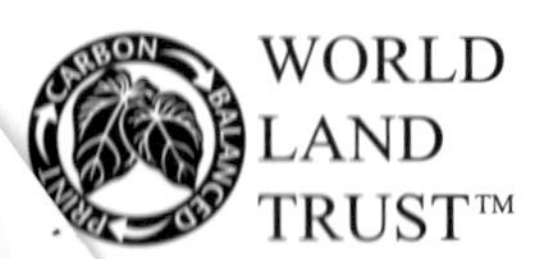

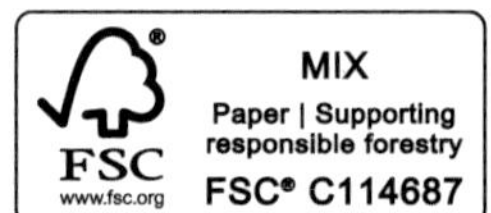

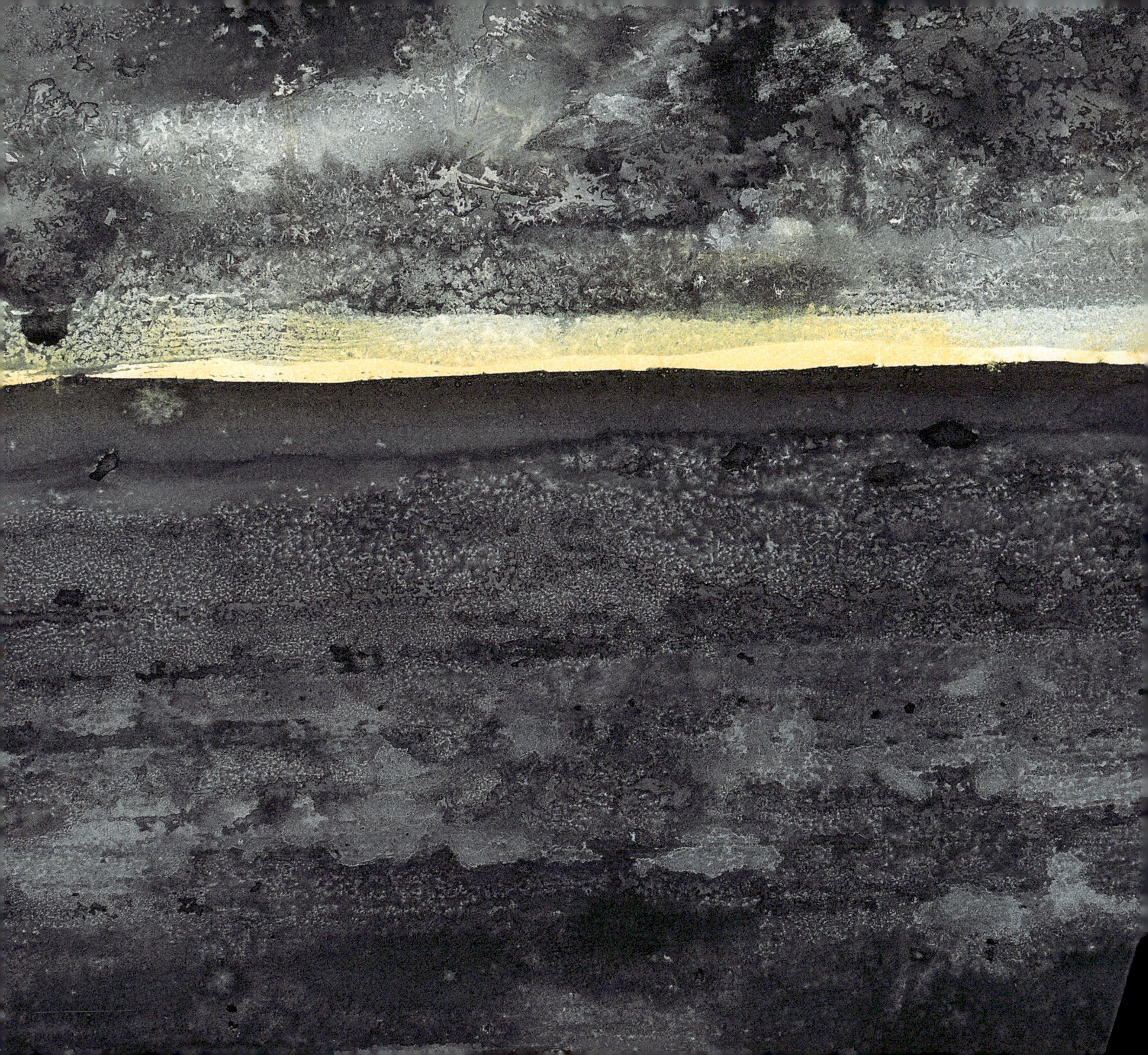